LIMITED WAR

Revisiting Kargil in the Indo-Pak conflict

D. Suba Chandran
Assistant Director
Institute of Peace and Conflict Studies

Program in Arms Control, Disarmament, and International Security
University of Illinois, Urbana-Champaign

India Research Press, New Delhi

India Research Press
B-4/22, Safdarjung Enclave, New Delhi – 110 029.
Ph.: 4694610; Fax : 4618637
www.indiaresearchpress.com
e-mail : bahrisons@vsnl.com

ISBN : 81-87943-81-5

LIMITED WAR - Revisiting Kargil in the Indo-Pak conflict
D. Suba Chandran 2005©® India Research Press, New Delhi

Includes bibliographical references.
1. Security - India / Pakistan 2. Politics - India / Pakistan .
3. War - India / Pakistan 3. South Asia - Politics. 4. South Asia - Security.
5. South Asia – War.
I. Title. II. Author

This ACDIS *Research Report* simultaneously Published 2005 as ACDIS//ACDIS CHAN:1.2004 University of Illinois at Urbana–Champaign

Series editor: Matthew A. Rosenstein

This book is published by India Research Press with the technical assistance of the Ford Foundation and is produced by *Suba Chandran* for the Program in Arms Control, Disarmament, and International Security at the University of Illinois, Urbana-Champaign.

Printed in India at Focus Impressions, New Delhi – 110 003..

For Prof. PR Chari
who encourages independent thinking and
appreciates alternate perceptions

Acknowledgments

Major General Dipankar Banerjee, currently Director of the Institute of Peace and Conflict Studies (IPCS), then Executive Director of the Regional Centre for Strategic Studies, was largely responsible for me undertaking this study at ACDIS. Had it not been for his support, I would have never ended up at ACDIS and had the opportunity to undertake this study. Professor P.R. Chari had no second thoughts in granting me leave from the IPCS office, thus also enabling me to undertake this study. His continuous encouragement has been a crucial factor in whatever I have achieved in the last few years.

Professor Cliff Singer gave me total freedom while I was researching at ACDIS. It was indeed a great experience attending his courses. Dr. Matt Rosenstein was an absolute pleasure to work with. He is the biggest walking database and all I needed to do was to request that he arrange for any appointment and the next day he would come to my room with his charming smile confirming it. Besides Matt, Sheila Roberts and Becky Osgood are two great administrative pillars, who made sure everything went smoothly for me, from getting my identification card upon arrival to the cab that finally took me to the Champaign airport. Jessica Moyer helped to get any reference material that I wanted, whether it was available at the ACDIS Library or outside. All of these individuals made my stay at ACDIS a great experience.

Gopi Rethinaraj and Kothavari Rajendran made sure that I never missed my South Indian food. They were always available for giving me a lift to the market and back and making sure I bought the right vegetables and other foodstuffs. Faisal Cheema was a great revelation and good company in Orchard Downs, which otherwise had every capability to bore one to death with its calm and quiet surroundings. On the positive side, Orchard Downs did teach both of us the virtues of cooking. Amit Gupta was always there with a smile to review my papers and chapters. Nasrullah Mirza, "the waterman," was literally "shining" with his presence and was always magnanimous in letting us use his kitchen. Lt. Col. Mark Bontrager and his wife along with their children gave us the much-needed homely atmosphere. There were numerous moments that will always remain evergreen amongst us.

Professor Stephen P. Cohen was kind enough to arrange for a meeting to discuss the draft of this paper at the Brookings Institution. He and Ambassador Teresita Schaffer enriched my understanding of limited war with their observations, insights, and probing questions. Professor Sumit Ganguly, Dr. David Cortright, Mr. Michael Vannoni, and Dr. Kent Biringer were kind enough to host me and find time to discuss my work.

Gen. V.P. Malik, a great human being—as I could observe from my limited interactions during his brief stay at Urbana-Champaign—provided me with much-needed insights into the Kargil War. His lecture on limited war at ACDIS was timely and useful for my study. Whatever differences I have in terms of perceiving limited war as an option to secure India's interests is a tribute to his resolve and determination during the Kargil War and his men.

Contents

D. Suba Chandran

Dr. Suba Chandran is Assistant Director of the Institute of Peace and Conflict Studies (IPCS), New Delhi. Currently he is a Visiting Fellow at the South Asia Strategic Stability unit (SASSU) at the University of Bradford. Earlier he was a Visiting Fellow at the Program in Arms Control, Disarmament, and International Security (ACDIS) at the University of Illinois at Urbana-Champaign, where he undertook this study.

He is working on *India's Security Problematique* at IPCS, and is also researching jointly with Rizwan Zeb, a Pakistani scholar, on *Creating Ripe Conditions to Resolve Indo-Pak Conflicts* as part of a Regional Centre for Strategic Studies Mahb-ul-Haq award. Chandran earned his Ph.D. at Jawaharlal Nehru University, New Delhi, and his M.A. and M.Phil. at Madras Christian College, Chennai.

Chandran's research interests include Pakistan, Kashmir, and suicide terrorism. Some of his recent publications include the co-edited volumes *Terrorism Post 9/11: An Indian Perspective* (New Delhi: Manohar Publishers, 2003); *Terrorism and its Repercussions on International Politics* (New Delhi: IPCS and FES, 2003); and *Missing Boundaries: Refugees, Migrants, Stateless Persons and IDPs in South Asia* (New Delhi: Manohar Publishers, 2003)

CHAPTER ONE
Limited War Theory
Origin and Growth

British military historian and strategist Sir Basil Henry Liddell Hart was the first to propound the idea of "limiting" wars when World War II was at its peak. He is considered "the apostle of limited war," but his arguments for limiting wars were different from those that were advocated in the mid-1950s in the United States.[1] According to Liddell Hart, "the more 'total' the war became, the greater the risk that 'freedom' would be permanently lost."[2]

Liddell Hart was not advocating limited war as a strategy, but was arguing that the wars should be limited. Two specific developments forced Liddell Hart to argue for limiting war. The first were the advancements in "automatic warfare," which he believed is far more destructive than earlier forms of war.[3] For him,

> The advent of "automatic warfare" should make plain the absurdity of warfare as a means of deciding nations' claims to superiority...They can no longer claim that war is any test of people's

1. Robert H. Larson, "B.H. Liddell Hart: Apostle of Limited War," *Military Affairs* 44, no. 2 (April 1980): 70-74.
2. Brian Bond, *Liddell Hart: A Study of His Military Thought* (New Brunswick, NJ: Rutgers University Press, 1977), 126.
3. By "automatic warfare," Liddell Hart meant the scientific development in the field of pilotless planes, which he called "flying bombs," and long-range rockets, which according to him have torn away the "veil of illusion that had so long obscured the reality of change in warfare—from a fight to a process of devastation. Being palpably 'inhuman' instruments, they inspired the feeling—which counts more than a truth apprehended by reason—that war is no longer a matter of *fighting*." See B.H. Liddell Hart, *The Revolution in Warfare* (New Haven, CT: Yale University Press, 1947), 36.

> fitness, or even its national strength. Science has undermined the foundations of nationalism, at the very time when the spirit of nationalism is most rampant.[4]

Second, there was the development of atomic weapons. Liddell Hart believed that "where both sides possess atomic power, total warfare makes nonsense" and any unlimited war "waged with atomic power would make worse than nonsense; it would be mutually suicidal."[5] He believed that there would be no victory to any side in an era where the use of atomic weapons was being contemplated. According to him, any total war, or "even the preparation for it, is likely to carry more evils in its train, without bearing any good promise in the event of victory."[6]

Liddell Hart wanted to "revive a code of limiting rules for warfare—based on a realistic view that wars are likely to occur again, and that the limitation of their destructiveness is to everybody's interest."[7] However, the arguments favoring limited war in the 1950s had different perceptions. In fact, the very definition of limited war underwent a considerable change in the 1950s.

Defining Limited War

What is limited war? What makes strategists consider a war "limited?"

A cursory look at the available definitions reveals not only the differences in perceptions of limited war but also the narrowness of their applicability. Invariably, the existing literature on the subject is written in the West, especially in the

---

4. Hart, *The Revolution in Warfare*, 37.
5. Ibid., 99.
6. Liddell Hart, quoted in Bond, *Liddell Hart: A Study of His Military Thought*, 164.
7. Hart, *The Revolution in Warfare*, 114.

United States. The principal focus of the definitions seems to be on "almost any military action that does not threaten the *immediate* destruction of the United States and the NATO powers, on the one hand, and the Soviet Union (including its Eastern Empire) and Communist China, on the other."[8] Limited war is defined as:

> One in which the belligerents restrict the purposes for which they fight to concrete, well defined objectives that do not demand the utmost military effort of which the belligerents are capable and that can be accommodated in a negotiated settlement...The battle is confined to a local geographical area and directed against selected targets—primarily those of direct military importance. It demands of the belligerents only a fractional commitment of their human and physical resources. It permits their economic, social and political patterns of existence to continue without serious disruption.[9]

Limited wars "were to be fought for ends far short of the complete subordination of one state's will to another's using means that involve far less than the total military resources of the belligerents and leave the civilian life and the armed forces of the belligerents largely intact."[10]

It meant that "either the ends or means, or both, are limited in the conflict."[11] Limited war is also defined as a "military encounter" in which the two warring sides "see each other on opposing sides and in which the effort of each falls short of the attempt to use all of its power to destroy the other."[12]

---

8. Seymour J. Deitchman, *Limited War and American Defense Policy* (Cambridge, MA: The MIT Press, 1964), 13.
9. Robert E. Osgood, *Limited War: The Challenge to American Strategy* (Chicago: The University of Chicago Press, 1957), 1-2.
10. Robert E. Osgood, *Limited War Revisited* (Boulder, CO: Westview Press, 1979), 3.
11. Christopher M. Gacek, *The Logic of Force: The Dilemma of Limited War in American Foreign Policy* (New York: Columbia University Press, 1994), 16.
12. Morton H. Halperin, *Limited War in the Nuclear Age* (New York: John Wiley & Sons, Inc., 1963), 2.

It may be a "war confined to a defined geographic area, or war that does not utilize the entire available weapons system (such as refraining from the use of thermonuclear weapons). It may be a war which utilizes the entire weapons system but it limits its employment to specific targets. But none of these military definitions seems adequate...In short, there exists no way to define a limited war in purely military terms."[13]

Based on the above definitions, a limited war involves the following:

- Military confrontation between two belligerents with concrete and well-defined objectives
- Both belligerents believe that such a military confrontation can be confined geographically and have minimal impact on civilians
- Such a military confrontation does not demand maximum military efforts

Limited War: Origin and Growth

The current perception of limited war originated during the cold war.[14] Amongst the two main actors of the cold war, it was in the United States that the concept of limited war became prominent as a political and military strategy vis-à-vis the former Soviet Union. Though the concept of limited war originated mainly as a limited conventional war in the 1950s and '60s, it expanded to include limited nuclear war in the 1970s. Limited war as a theory evolved both as an offensive and defensive strategy to protect the strategic interests of the

---

13. Henry Kissinger, *Nuclear Weapons and Foreign Policy* (New York: Council on Foreign Relations, 1957), 139.
14. See the following: Deitchman, *Limited War and American Defense Policy;* Halperin, *Limited War in the Nuclear Age*; Osgood, *Limited War: The Challenge to American Strategy;* Osgood, *Limited War Revisited.*

United States. As an offensive strategy, limited war was part of the US strategy to deal with the Soviet Union; as a defensive strategy, it aimed to protect the interests of the United States and its allies, especially in Europe.

Replacing Maximum Retaliation

In the 1950s, with the ascendancy of weapons of mass destruction and the decline of political use of war as an instrument, the United States was searching for a new strategy vis-à-vis the Soviet Union. The question was: how to deter the Soviet Union, which had already broken the nuclear monopoly of the United States and "acquired a significant nuclear armory and the capacity to retaliate against the Unites States homeland?"[15] The first major strategy was that of massive retaliation. By the mid 1950s, even while the strategy of massive retaliation evolved, Bernard Brodie and William Kaufmann refuted the utility of massive retaliation as a strategy to deal with the Soviet Union.[16] Writing in 1956, Kaufmann observed:

> It is by no means clear, even now, that we can destroy the centers of Soviet or Chinese power without having a similar catastrophe visited upon us; and certainly within a very short time we will have to accept the idea of parity of capabilities for mutual extinction.[17]

Henry Kissinger was one of the first strategists to understand this growing dilemma related to weapons of mass destruction and their political and military implications in case of an all-out war. He wrote in 1957,

---

15. John Garnett, "Limited War," in *Contemporary Strategy: Theory and Practice*, eds. John Baylis et al. (New York: Holmes & Meier Publishers, 1975), 115.
16. See Bernard Brodie, *Strategy in the Missile Age* (Princeton, NJ: Princeton University Press, 1959); William W. Kaufmann, "Limited Warfare," in *Military Policy and National Security*, eds. William W. Kaufmann et al. (Princeton, NJ: Princeton University Press, 1956), 102-136
17. Kaufmann, "Limited Warfare," 106.

> As the power of modern weapons grows, the threat of all-out war loses its credibility and therefore its political effectiveness. Our capacity for massive retaliation did not avert the Korean War, the loss of northern Indo-China, the Soviet-Egyptian arms deal, or the Suez crisis. A deterrent which one is afraid to implement when it is challenged ceases to be a deterrent.[18]

The main question that faced strategists was: What if the strategies of massive conventional or nuclear retaliation or threats of its use fail to deter the adversary? By the second half of the 1950s, US strategists realized that with the presence of nuclear weapons with the United States, the threat of using them as a part of their massive retaliation strategy failed to achieve US objectives. Kissinger, who led this school of thought against the strategy of massive retaliation argued,

> Every increase in destructiveness is purchased at the price of reduced credibility of the retaliatory threat. In this vicious circle, deterrence may fail. If it does, the reliance on massive retaliation will not guarantee the direct outcome. It will lead either to surrender or to the most catastrophic form of war.[19]

The existing strategy was not working; hence a new strategy was needed to achieve US strategic objectives vis-à-vis the Soviet Union.

In Kissinger's words, such a strategy should enable the United States "to avoid the dilemma of having a choice between all-out war and a gradual loss of positions, between Armageddon and defeat without war."[20] It was under these conditions that limited wars were seen as possessing a "number of other virtues," though "they may not be adequate substitutes for victory."[21]

---

18. Kissinger, *Nuclear Weapons and Foreign Policy*, 134.
19. Henry Kissinger, *The Necessity of Choice: Prospects of American Foreign Policy* (New York: Anchor Books, 1962), 59.
20. Kissinger, *Nuclear Weapons and Foreign Policy*, 136.
21. Kaufmann, "Limited Warfare," 106.

The virtues of a limited war were explained by Kaufmann:

> They enable us to escape frcm having to choose between retreat and the nuclear holocaust. They preserve us from the revolutionary and disorienting charges that are the products of great wars. They offer the prospect of bringing military means and policy aims into much closer relationship than they have enjoyed for many years. And limited warfare affords all these benefits, not at a trifling cost by any manner of any means, but at a cost far smaller than a modern nuclear conflict would entail.[22]

The "Twin Fears"

Limited war as a defensive strategy arose to defend the interests of the United States and those of its allies against what Robert Osgood calls the "twin fears."[23] According to him,

> The United States and to lesser degrees major US democratic allies (except where they were directly involved) feared that local wars might become instruments of communist expansion that could not be contained; indigenous local resistance would be inadequate, and US intervention would either be ineffective in shoring up weak governments or entail too big a risk of Soviet or Chinese counter intervention and nuclear war. Second there was also the fear that US nuclear forces might prove an ineffective deterrent; the growth of the Soviet capacity to devastate the Unites States and its allies would erode the credibility of the US nuclear intervention or retaliation.[24]

Maintaining US credibility in Europe was a critical component of the limited war strategy. How credible was the US support to its allies in case of a Soviet attack in Europe? Should the United States be willing to risk the lives of Americans or cities such as Chicago or New York in return for an attack carried out in Europe? John Garnett phrased the

---

22. Ibid., 107.
23. Osgood, *Limited War Revisited*, 5.
24. Ibid., 4-5.

European dilemma eloquently: "threatening the Soviet Union with massive retaliation even for a relatively minor aggression in Europe lacked all credibility when the consequences of implementing the threat were likely to result in the complete destruction of the American way of life." He quoted French General Pierre-Marie Gallois: "No nation can be expected to commit suicide for the sake of another."[25]

The strategic parity that the Soviet Union acquired with the United States, in terms of the "Soviet capacity to devastate the United States with nuclear weapons" and the fear of erosion of the US ability to "use nuclear weapons to protect even its important allies, if they could not be protected conventionally"[26] became two main reasons for the origin of the concept of limited war.

Objectives of Limited War

What are the objectives of a limited war? Who defines these objectives? Are they limited or unlimited? And, how limited can these objectives be?

According to Kissinger, a limited war "is fought for specific political objectives, which by their existence, tend to establish a relationship between the force employed and the goal to be attained. It reflects an attempt to affect the opponent's will not to crush it, to make the conditions imposed seem more attractive than continued resistance, to strive for specific goals and not for complete annihilation."[27] And these objectives should be minimal and "hold the conflict within the desired limits."[28]

---

25. Garnett, "Limited War," 116.
26. Osgood, *Limited War Revisited*, 15.
27. Kissinger, *Nuclear Weapons and Foreign Policy*, 140.
28. Kaufmann, "Limited Warfare," 113.

Morton Halperin believed that the United States and the Soviet Union could fight a limited war for three objectives—basic foreign policy objectives, political-effects objectives, and battlefield objectives.[29]

Foreign Policy Political Objectives

The first political objective was the protection of US interests, especially in Europe. As mentioned earlier, US allies in Europe needed to be assured of the utility and effectiveness of US strategy. Any negative impact on this would have a demonstrative effect in other parts of the world and would erode US influence.

Second in importance was the prevention of Soviet influence over other communist and non-communist countries. When the cold war began, containing the Soviet Union was the main issue before the US policy makers. While some preferred massive retaliation, others preferred limited retaliation. Giving three reasons for developing a strategy of limited war, Kissinger wrote in 1957, "First, limited war represents the only means for preventing the Soviet bloc, at an acceptable cost, from overrunning the peripheral areas of Eurasia."[30] Accordingly, it was believed that a limited war strategy, more than a threat of total nuclear war, was likely to contain the Soviet Union.

Third, besides containing the Soviet Union, it was also believed that a limited war would also break the monolithic nature of the Soviet bloc. Kissinger forecasted,

---

29. Halperin, *Limited War in the Nuclear Age*, 3.
30. The other two reasons according to him are that "a wide range of military capabilities may spell the difference between defeat and victory even in all-out war. Finally, intermediate applications of our power offer the best chance to bring about strategic changes favorable to our side." Kissinger, *Nuclear Weapons and Foreign Policy*, 147.

> The USSR may be forced to loosen its hold on its European satellites if it finds that the effort to hold them in line absorbs even more of its strength. And relations between China and the Soviet Union may become cooler if the alliance forces either partner to shoulder risks for objectives which are of no benefit to it. Tito's break with Moscow was caused at least in part by his disenchantment over the Soviet Union's lukewarm support on the Trieste issue, and that in turn was due to the unwillingness of the Kremlin to risk an all-out war for the sake of peripheral objective. Similarly it is not clear how much China would risk to rescue the USSR from embarrassments in Europe or in the Middle East, or to what lengths the USSR is prepared to go to increase the power of China in Asia.[31]

Fourth, it was believed that a limited war would have a demonstration effect. The side that is willing to risk a limited war aims to demonstrate its seriousness to its adversary and the actual use of force or the threat of use of force is primarily to prove that it would not hesitate to use force to secure its objectives. The threat of force by the United States during the Cuban missile crisis is considered as an example for such a motivation. The United States was "partly motivated by the feeling that it was important to use force and risk a nuclear war in order to secure its objectives. The United States acted to convince Khrushchev that the Kennedy administration was not too liberal to fight when it felt its rights were threatened." Besides proving a point to the adversary, the demonstration effect also must take into account other countries in the region where the limited war is planned. It was believed that "the manner in which the United States responds to Communist aggression in Indo-China, for example, affects the orientation of Thailand, the Philippines, and other Asian nations."[32]

Fifth, it was believed that limited wars were essential for

---

31. Kissinger, *Nuclear Weapons and Foreign Policy*, 148.
32. Halperin, *Limited War in the Nuclear Age*, 5.

ensuring that deterrence could actually work. Kissinger, a leading exponent of this argument, considered "the purpose of a strategy of limited war is first, to strengthen deterrence and second, if deterrence should fail, to provide an opportunity for settlement before the automatism of the retaliatory forces takes over."[33] The argument is two fold. One, limited war enhances deterrence. Two, if deterrence fails, limited war then "provides another opportunity for both sides to prevent a catastrophe."[34]

According to Kissinger, "deterrence is greatest when military strength is coupled with the willingness to employ it. It is achieved when one side's readiness to run risks in retaliation to the other is high; it is least effective when the willingness to run risks is low, no matter how powerful the military capability."[35] The belief then was that the presence of strategic weapons, including nuclear ones, need not necessarily bring deterrence; rather, it was the threat or the actual use of force that would deter the adversary. Therefore, deterrence needed to be "supplemented" by another strategy, otherwise the "Western alliance could fall victim to Soviet salami tactics—a series of hostile acts which, considered individually, were not sufficiently serious to justify massive retaliation."[36]

Kissinger links deterrence with limited war. In his later work, he makes this linkage explicit: "A strategy of limited war would seek to achieve deterrence not so much through the threat of devastation but through depriving the aggressor of the possibility of gaining his objective."[37]

---

33. Kissinger, *The Necessity of Choice*, 61-62.
34. Ibid., 64.
35. Kissinger, *Nuclear Weapons and Foreign Policy*, 132.
36. Garnett, "Limited War," 116.
37. Kissinger, *The Necessity of Choice*, 61.

The main issue was how to make the adversary believe that one is serious and how to convince its political leadership that one could use force, though it might lead to a stalemate. Given this dilemma, the advocates of this argument believed "given the power of modern weapons, a nation that relies on all-out war as its chief deterrent imposes a fearful psychological handicap on itself. The most agonizing decision a statesman can face is whether or not to unleash all-out war; all pressures will make for hesitation, short of a direct attack threatening the national existence."[38]

The critics of limited war, however, did not agree with the assumption that limited war would assure deterrence. If massive destruction was not the desired objective of such a strategy, either through massive retaliation or otherwise, then limited war could induce the states to wage a war. To this extent, limited war was seen as dangerous since it undermined, rather than complemented, the deterrence strategy.[39]

Military Objectives: Are There Any?

Could there be any military objectives in a limited war? What role does the military play in a limited war scenario? Kissinger finds that a limited war, being "essentially a limited act," presents a dilemma to the military. The objectives of an all-out war are easy to define as "the limits set by military considerations and even by military capacity. The targets for an all-out war are fixed, and the force requirements are determined by the need to assemble overwhelming power. The characteristic of a limited war, on the other hand, is the existence of ground rules, which define the relationship of military to political objectives."[40]

---

38. Kissinger, *Nuclear Weapons and Foreign Policy*, 133.
39. Garnett, "Limited War," 117.
40. Kissinger, *Nuclear Weapons and Foreign Policy*, 140.

What role does military power play then in the event of a limited war? Osgood argues that it "should be subordinate to national policy" and "the only legitimate purpose of military forces is to serve the nation's political objective."[41] Clearly this is based on the famous dictum of Karl von Clausewitz that "war is nothing but a continuation of political intercourse with an admixture of other means."[42]

The role of military power is limited, but crucial. If one is to go by Clausewitz's dictum, then success in a war depends on the political utilization of the war and not on defeating the enemy in the battleground. However a "measure of military success is the necessary condition for achieving the political objectives of war."[43]

Internal Political Objectives

Internal political objectives also need to be considered. Once a limited war starts, both sides would be equally concerned about the level of domestic support to the war and its eventual outcome. Unlike during a full-fledged war, internal support from various political actors—especially the main opposition party and the general population—for the limited war would not be spontaneous and not subject to criticism. While the general population may like the war to be taken to its logical conclusion of suppression of the enemy forces, they would be unwilling to accept any defeat. The pressure then would be on the state, so as not to lose the limited war. It was believed in the United States that "the decision to expand a local war will be influenced not only by the reactions of other political actors and the American electorate, but also by the

---

41. Osgood, *Limited War: The Challenge to American Strategy*, 13.
42. Karl von Clausewitz, *On War*, trans. O.J. Matthijs Jolles (New York: The Modern Library, 1943).
43. Osgood, *Limited War: The Challenge to American Strategy*, 13.

major domestic goals of the Administration itself, on which its political life also depends."[44]

Limited War: Who Defines the Objectives?

It is clear that the main objectives of a limited war are political and not military. This partly answers the second question raised in the beginning of this section—who defines the objectives of a limited war? Since a limited war is not fought for purely military objectives or to arrive at a military solution, the "political leadership must...assume the responsibility for defining the framework, within which the military are to develop their plans and capabilities. To demand of the military that they set their own limits is to set in motion a vicious cycle."[45]

The political leadership should define the objectives of a limited war, since the "whole conduct of warfare—its strategy, its tactics, its termination—must be governed by the nature of a nation's political objectives and not by independent standards of military success or glory."[46] Kissinger argues:

> The purpose of limited war is to inflict losses or to pose risks for the enemy out of proportion to the objectives under dispute. The more moderate the objective, the less violent the war is likely to be. This does not mean that the military operations cannot go beyond the territory or the objective in dispute; indeed, one way of increasing the enemy's willingness to settle is to deprive him of something he can regain only by making peace.[47]

What Limits a Limited War?

What are the main factors that could have convinced the

---

44. Halperin, *Limited War in the Nuclear Age*, 25.
45. Kissinger, *Nuclear Weapons and Foreign Policy*, 141.
46. Osgood, *Limited War: The Challenge to American Strategy*, 22.
47. Kissinger, *Nuclear Weapons and Foreign Policy*, 145.

advocates of limited war to believe that wars could be limited? Why should an adversary limit its response in a war when it is not going in its favor? What would limit the side that has initiated the conflict, if the limited offensive is not sufficient enough to achieve its initial objectives?

In the event a limited war, it is believed that the strategic interests of the belligerents at the global level would keep the conflict limited. Though a limited war would be initiated to achieve some of the above mentioned objectives, its expansion would be considered against global interests. Since a limited war is considered to be a means to achieve the global objectives, the latter, it is believed, would keep the former from escalating.

> Each side will be conscious of the possible impact of a local war on its efforts to reach accommodation in other geographic areas or on other problems. In 1954, for example, the Sino-Soviet bloc was about to launch a peace offensive which would have been embarrassed by the continuation of expansion of war in Indochina. Similarly in 1958 when East and West were beginning to clash over Berlin, they were at the same time attempting to negotiate a treaty to ban nuclear tests. The successful conclusion of these negotiations would have been highly unlikely in the event of armed conflict on the European continent.[48]

As long as the wars take place in the periphery, the superpowers would keep the war limited, as there is no need to risk a total war. It is believed that the United States kept the war in Korea limited so that it could "maintain a favorable posture in the event of a more direct challenge in a more important region."[49]

Second, it is also believed that the "reluctance of the major powers to commit resources that may be required to deal with

48. Halperin, *Limited War in the Nuclear Age*, 6.
49. Bernard Brodie, "Some Notes on the Evolution of Air Doctrine," *World Politics* 7, no. 3 (April 1955): 369.

other areas of potential violence or to deter central war"[50] would keep the war in a region limited. This is based on the belief that there are a number of potential areas all over the world, where a side would have to engage the other in a limited conflict, hence spending all its energy in one area is not prudent. Both sides are aware of this limitation, hence would not expand the limited war in to a central war.

Kissinger states that "the restraint which keeps a war limited is a psychological one; the consequences of a limited victory or a limited defeat or a stalemate—the three possible outcomes of a limited war—must seem preferable to the consequences of an all-out war...Limited war, therefore, involves as many psychological complexities as a policy of deterrence."[51]

Third, it is also believed that the cooperation between the two adversaries during a limited war would keep the war limited. Adversaries who would otherwise not like to cooperate, and who prefer a limited war, would however cooperate during actual conflict, so that it does not escalate. A complicated argument, nevertheless, was advanced by Kissinger:

> Limited war is based on a kind of tacit bargain not to exceed certain restraints. One side's desire to keep the war limited is of no avail unless the other side cooperates; it takes two to keep a limited war limited or a local defense local.[52]

Fourth, the limited war theorists advocates that the dangers of escalation would keep a war limited. Kissinger, identifying the contradiction in this argument, argued,

---

50. Halperin, *Limited War in the Nuclear Age*, 6-7.
51. Kissinger, *Nuclear Weapons and Foreign Policy*, 168-69.
52. Kissinger, *The Necessity of Choice*, 62.

> However paradoxical it may seem, the danger of escalation is one of the chief reasons why a strategy of limited war contributes to deterrence and also why, if deterrence fails, there is a chance of keeping a conflict limited. A strategy of limited war adds to deterrence for the very reason usually invoked against it... One side or both may be willing to accept limited defeat rather than take the initiative in breaching the rules and to act in a manner that reassures the other of such willingness. The rules may be respected because if they are once broken, there is no assurance that any new ones can be found and jointly recognized in time to check the widening of the conflict.[53]

Fifth, geography has an important role to play in limiting the war. The "physical configuration of Korea" limited the Korean War, as the "area was surrounded by water, and the principal northern political boundary was marked dramatically and unmistakably by a river."[54]

Overcoming the Dangers of Escalation

The advocates of limited war were aware of the implications of escalation. To overcome escalation, the opponents need to be persuaded on numerous aspects. Kaufmann asserted,

> (The enemy) would have to be persuaded that he could not achieve his objectives by the means currently being employed. He would also have to be convinced that he could not attain them by expanding the war in scope or in weapons. At the same time, within the existing framework of the contest, he would have to have it demonstrated that the costs of fighting to him outweighed the costs to the United States, and consequently that the advantages of terminating the conflict were greater than the advantages of continuing it.[55]

---

53. Thomas C. Schelling, "Bargaining, Communication and Limited War," *Conflict Resolution* 1, no. 1 (March 1957): 34.
54. Ibid., 33.
55. Kaufmann, "Limited Warfare," 113.

Halperin identified two kinds of escalation—inadvertent and deliberate.[56] Forces and events of war may spin out of control, ultimately leading to escalation, which is inadvertent. On the other hand, the side that may be losing could deliberately escalate the conflict, so as to avoid the defeat at the battlefield. "Not only may an adversary balk at giving signs of eagerness to come to agreement; it is even possible that one side in a potential war may have a tactical interest in keeping that war unrestrained and aggravating the likelihood of mutual destruction in case it comes."[57]

How is a war kept limited? Or what would keep a war limited between two sides and make sure that it is not escalated—either inadvertently or deliberately? What kept the Soviet Union and the United States from escalating the numerous local conflicts that took place between them?

According to Kissinger, limited war "presupposes three conditions: the ability to generate pressures other than the threat of all-out war; the ability to create a climate in which survival is not thought to be at stake in each issue; and the ability to keep control of public opinion in case a disagreement arises over whether national survival is at stake."[58]

The following are essential to overcome the dangers of escalation in a limited war scenario: limited objectives and a strategic doctrine, strategic parity, strategic stability, and strategic communication.

Limited Objectives and Strategic Doctrine

One essential aspect of keeping war limited is to have the

---

56. Halperin, *Limited War in the Nuclear Age*, 11.
57. Schelling, "Bargaining, Communication and Limited War," 35.
58. Kissinger, *Nuclear Weapons and Foreign Policy*, 170.

objectives limited. Bernard Brodie calls this "deliberate restraint."[59] Any unlimited objectives or objectives aiming at total destruction of the adversary—both politically and militarily—would escalate a limited war. Any attempt to "reduce the enemy to impotence would remove the psychological balance which makes it profitable for both sides to keep the war limited. Faced with the ultimate threat of complete defeat, the losing side may seek to deprive its opponent of the margin to impose his will by unleashing a thermonuclear holocaust."[60]

It is essential for the party that initiates the limited war to keep in mind its aim of limited victories—victories that are relative and not absolute. An absolute victory between two equal adversaries is impossible, given the ability to destroy the other completely and convincingly in any war scenario. Likewise, an absolute loss is impossible, given the ability to protect oneself from total destruction. Since neither total victory nor total loss is a likely outcome in any war situation, both sides should be willing to accept limited victory or limited failure.

To keep a war limited, then, the "deliberate restraint" must be "massive." For example, it should avoid strategic bombing of cities with nuclear weapons.[61] But how can the bombing be strategic, if the cities are to be avoided in a limited war scenario? Brodie explains the paradox:

> Limited war might conceivably include strategic bombing carried on in a selective or otherwise limited manner, for example bombing with nuclear weapons on selected targets such as airfields while

59. Bernard Brodie, *Strategy in the Missile Age* (Princeton, NJ: Princeton University Press, 1959), 309.
60. Kissinger, *Nuclear Weapons and Foreign Policy,* 145.
61. Brodie, *Strategy in the Missile Age,* 310.

> being as careful as possible not to hit cities. It is certainly conceivable that strategic bombing could be carried on in a restrained and discriminatory fashion.[62]

Limited war "cannot be a means of bringing about a radical alteration in the distribution of power; that would be a contradiction in terms. Nor can it be a method of obtaining overwhelmingly favorable resolutions of outstanding issues."[63] Limited war should aim at limited victory and "the terms must be short of unconditional surrender and give the vanquished a chance to negotiate on a reasonable basis."[64]

Kissinger explains the importance of a limited victory-limited failure outcome: "Limited war should not be considered a cheaper method of imposing unconditional surrender but an opportunity for another attempt to prevent a final showdown. We must enter it prepared to negotiate and to settle for something less that our traditional notion of complete victory."[65] Elsewhere he writes, "The concept of limited war and the diplomacy appropriate to it reflect the fact that in the nuclear age the possibility of total solutions no longer exists."[66]

Besides limiting the objectives, it is also essential to convey to the other side, both explicitly and implicitly, that the side that initiates the conflict does not intend to escalate the conflict into an all-out war. Diplomacy plays a vital role here, once the limited conflict has begun or is about to begin. Kissinger considered diplomacy the third necessary prerequisite of a

62. Ibid.
63. Kaufmann, "Limited Warfare," 127.
64. Bernard Brodie, "Unlimited Weapons and Limited War," *The Reporter* 11, no. 9 (November 18, 1954): 20.
65. Kissinger, *The Necessity of Choice*, 64.
66. Henry A. Kissinger, "Controls, Inspection and Limited War," *The Reporter* 16, no. 12 (June 13, 1957): 19.

limited war strategy.[67] In one article, Kissinger argued, "Even a unilateral declaration of what we understand by limited war would accomplish a great deal because it would provide a strong incentive to the Soviet Union to adopt a similar interpretation."[68]

Strategic Parity

For both sides not to escalate in a limited war scenario, it is essential that both sides have strategic parity, in terms of strategic weapons, deployment of troops, and even in terms of strategies. Both sides should be aware that an escalation would hurt them equally in economic, political, and strategic terms.

Is a limited war possible between adversaries that have no parity? In such a scenario, a war between them would always be limited. The stronger side is unlikely to use its full might to completely annihilate the weaker side. A war between a stronger and weaker power, either at the global or regional level would always be limited from one side, though it may appear unlimited from the other side. A war between the United States and Cuba or between India and Bangladesh is always likely to be limited.

Though theoretically it is possible that the weaker side uses all its forces and prepares for a total annihilation of itself against a stronger side, historically such a war has never taken place. The weaker side has always acknowledged the superiority of the stronger side sooner or later and brought an end to the war. The rhetoric of fighting until the last man

67. According to Kissinger, the strategy of limited war "must be coupled with a diplomacy which succeeds in conveying that all-out war is not the sole response to aggression and that there exists a willingness to negotiate a settlement short of unconditional surrender." Kissinger, *The Necessity of Choice*, 67.
68. Kissinger, "Controls, Inspection and Limited War," 17.

standing has actually never taken place. Neither are there examples in the recent past that suggest that a stronger side wished for total annihilation of its weaker adversary.

Strategic Stability

Can a limited war take place between two adversaries who have parity but no strategic stability? Limited war theorists like Halperin believe that limited war can take place even during periods of strategic instability. According to them, "Should a local war occur in a period of strategic instability, both of the major powers will probably seek to minimize their stake in the war so that no outcome will appear to affect their basic relationship in ways that make the dangers of an explosion more likely...With both sides alert to the danger of inducing a preemptive attack, the local war is likely to remain at low key while both sides refrain from expansionist actions such as the introduction of nuclear weapons or the crossing of an international border which will heighten the tension and the expectations that an explosion is imminent."[69]

Halperin also believes that an "unstable strategic balance is also likely to provide profitable payoffs for a side willing to take risks. Faced with a *fait accompli,* the defending side is likely to be inhibited from joining the battle in a situation of unstable deterrence. Thus, if local military action does not lead to preemption, it is also not likely to lead to intervention. An unstable strategic balance, then, is likely to reduce the danger of local war and central war by expansion, if both sides act cautiously."[70]

Strategic Communication

It is also essential to communicate to the other side the extent

---

69. Halperin, *Limited War in the Nuclear Age,* 12.
70. Ibid., 12-13.

to which one would go in a limited war situation. Communication is an essential prerequisite to keep war limited; the lack of it could expand a conflict.[71]

Why should the belligerents communicate? It is believed "the greater the costs and risks of a military measure, actual or contemplated, the greater the tendency for the men at the higher levels of government to talk and act as if they were guided by the academic theory of limited war."[72] Communication is essential off the battlefield, as the opponent "must be given to understand what constitutes the risks of changing the rules of the game and what are the conditions of terminating the conflict."[73]

Communication is also essential to make the opponent understand the limited objectives of the other side in a limited war situation. The failure to convey this message would in fact escalate the conflict. If side A believes that the objective of B, which has initiated the conflict, are more than what B actually has in mind, then A would retaliate more then what B had expected. Since B was not planning to use much force initially and since A is involved in a response that would negate the objectives of B, B would also be forced to increase the conflict level.

Communication also has a "symbolic" value during a conflict situation, for "it signifies both a reluctance to permit the conflict to get out of hand and a willingness always to consider a settlement of the dispute."[74]

---

71. Schelling, "Bargaining, Communication and Limited War," 19-36; Kissinger, *The Necessity of Choice*, 63.
72. Stephen Peter Rosen, "Vietnam and the American Theory of Limited War," *International Security* 7, no. 2 (autumn 1982): 88.
73. Kaufmann, "Limited Warfare," 123.
74. Ibid.

Both the United States and the Soviet Union, irrespective of the cold war, kept the communication channels open and were engaged throughout at different levels. Both superpowers were "engaged in a continuous series of interdependent exchanges, in which the stakes, i.e, payoffs, and the moves of players are defined by their mutually expected behavior in pursuit of shared and conflicting values and interests."[75] Irrespective of their differences and conditions of "imperfect conditions," both superpowers were willing to "coordinate their moves for mutual, if not equal, advantage."[76]

In retrospect, the cold war was also viewed as cooperation, especially on regional relations. Edward A. Kolodziej comments that he was

> ...struck by the number, variety, and accumulation of understandings, some explicit but more frequently tacit, that have been relied upon by elites in Moscow and Washington in shaping their initiatives and responses to the behavior and policies of their rivals and in managing their mutual conflicts.[77]

It would even be better if the adversaries have a clear military doctrine, which is communicated to the other side, so that there is no inadvertent escalation in case of a limited war. However, Halperin argues that such a clear military doctrine is not an essential prerequisite for a limited war. According to him, "prior to 1957, the United States had no such doctrine and yet it engaged in a number of limited military encounters, including the Korean War. Little is known about esoteric Soviet doctrine on local wars...Certainly there has been no explicit

75. Edward A. Kolodziej, "The Cold War as Cooperation," in *The Cold War as Cooperation: Superpower Cooperation in Regional Conflict Management*, eds. Roger E. Kanet and Edward A. Kolodziej (London: Macmillan, 1991), 6.
76. Ibid.
77. Ibid., 7.

exchange of attitudes between the United States and the Soviet Union on the possibility of limiting local wars."[78]

The Primacy of Politics and a Limited Role for the Military

The main objective of a limited war should be political and not military, if escalation is to be kept under check. Consequently, the decisions should be made by the political leadership and not by the military.

What role should the military play? According to Stephen Rosen, "The military should *not* be given a free hand, but they must be allowed the freedom to solve the military problem within the limits set for them. The military will be able to begin solving the problem only after it receives meaningful instructions and parameters. The military itself should be staffed at the highest levels with men who have demonstrated the ability to command and adapt to difficult circumstances in combat and who are respected for that ability within the army."[79]

To conclude, limited war as a strategy in the US security calculus emerged during the 1950s primarily as an alternative to massive retaliation. Since an all-out war could neither be fought nor won during the cold war, the strategists in the United States perceived limited war as an answer in their country's search for a new strategy vis-à-vis the Soviet Union.

Second, the concept of limited war emerged mainly as an instrument of securing US political interests, mainly in terms of preventing the spread of Soviet influence outside Eastern Europe and breaking the monolithic nature of the Soviet bloc. There were little or no military objectives in limited war scenarios.

---

78. Halperin, *Limited War in the Nuclear Age*, 15.
79. Rosen, "Vietnam and the American Theory of Limited War," 112.

Third, it was believed that the strategic interests of the superpowers at the global level, reluctance to commit all the resources in one area where the limited war was to take place, dangers of escalation, and limited cooperation amongst the adversaries would keep the war limited.

Finally, strategic parity, strategic stability, and strategic communication were seen as three crucial factors in any limited war situation.

CHAPTER TWO
India's Limited War
In Search of a New Strategy?

The idea of India engaging in a limited war with Pakistan evolved following the Kargil conflict in 1998. Why did such a concept emerge? What are the main arguments for the utility of limited war advanced by its advocates?

Although the concept of a limited war between India and Pakistan gathered momentum in the post-Kargil conflict period, the idea is not new. Since the 1980s, there have been a number of inferences to its possibility on the subcontinent. Though India has been advocating it since the late 1990s, and Pakistan rejecting it, ironically it is Pakistan that first floated the concept in the 1980s.

Limited War with Pakistan: Looking for a New Strategy

As in the case of the United States versus the Soviet Union during the 1950s, the idea of limited war gained currency while Indian defense planners were scouting for a new strategy to deal with Pakistan in the post-Kargil security environment. Indian Defence Minister George Fernandes, while explaining the doctrine of limited war, argued for the need for a new policy:

> India has traditionally pursued a non-aggressive, non-provocative defence policy based on the philosophy of defensive defence. This represents the political doctrine of employing military power. But military efficiency will continue to demand the pursuit of the principle that "offence is the best means of defence."[1]

---

1. George Fernandes, "The Dynamics of Limited War," *Strategic Affairs* (October 16, 2000), http://www.stratmag.com/ issueOct-15/page07.htm.

Since the 1990s, India's political efforts to secure peace with Pakistan failed to make any major breakthroughs, despite occasional promising developments. Inside Jammu and Kashmir, though the intensity of militancy waxed and waned, peace still remained distant, irrespective of elections for state and national legislative assemblies.

Three major factors in the late 1990s aided the emergence of limited war as a strategy to deal with Pakistan. First was the failure of any sustained political dialogue with Pakistan, leading to an acceptable compromise on all issues including Jammu and Kashmir. Second was the emergence of militancy in Jammu and Kashmir and its continuance, irrespective of India's efforts to combat it. Third was the Kargil War itself, which was perceived by a section in India as a limited war under the nuclear umbrella.

Failure of Political Dialogue

The idea of limited war became prominent after the failure by India to reach any political understanding with Pakistan. There were meetings at the foreign secretary level, summits between the prime ministers of India and Pakistan, secret meetings between the emissaries of the two governments, numerous confidence and security building measures, and many attempts at the track-II level.

Between 1989 and 1998, there were twelve rounds of talks at the foreign secretary level and two rounds of talks by the prime ministers, besides numerous meetings at other levels.[2] Of particular importance was the failure of the talks at the foreign secretary level in 1998 and that of the Lahore process in 1999.

---

2. For a report and analysis of the various meetings at the foreign secretary level, see J.N. Dixit, *India-Pakistan in War & Peace* (London: Routledge, 2002).

Table 2.1: Meetings between the Prime Minister of India and the Prime Minister/President of Pakistan since 1972

Date	Venue	India	Pakistan	Occasion/ Outcome
July 1972	Simla	Indira Gandhi	Zulfikar Ali Bhutto	Simla Agreement
31 Aug 1978	Nairobi	Morarji Desai	Zia ul-Haq	Jomo Kenyatta's funeral
18 Apr 1980	Salisbury	Indira Gandhi	Zia ul-Haq	Zimbabwe's independence
01 Nov 1982	New Delhi	Indira Gandhi	Zia ul-Haq	Decision to establish a Indo-Pak Joint Commission
10 Mar 1983	New Delhi	Indira Gandhi	Zia ul-Haq	7th NAM Summit
04 Nov 1984	New Delhi	Rajiv Gandhi	Zia ul-Haq	Indira Gandhi's funeral
13 Mar 1985	Moscow	Rajiv Gandhi	Zia ul-Haq	Konstantin Chernenko's funeral
23 Oct 1985	New York	Rajiv Gandhi	Zia ul-Haq	UN General Assembly Meeting
18 Nov 1985	Oman	Rajiv Gandhi	Zia ul-Haq	Oman's 10th anniversary
07 Dec 1985	Dhaka	Rajiv Gandhi	Zia ul-Haq	SAARC Summit
17 Dec 1985	New Delhi	Rajiv Gandhi	Zia ul-Haq	Summit on Indo-Pak relations
15 Mar 1986	Stockholm	Rajiv Gandhi	Mohd Khan Junejo	Olaf Palme's Funeral
17 Nov 1986	Bangalore	Rajiv Gandhi	Mohd Khan Junejo	SAARC Summit
21 Feb 1987	New Delhi	Rajiv Gandhi	Zia ul-Haq	Cricket match in Jaipur

04 Nov 1987	Kathmandu	Rajiv Gandhi	Mohd Khan Junejo	SAARC Summit
20 Aug 1988	Islamabad	Venkataraman (President)	Ghulam Ishaq Khan	Zia's funeral
29-31 Dec 1988	Islamabad	Rajiv Gandhi	Benazir Bhutto	SAARC Summit
Jul 1989	Islamabad	Rajiv Gandhi	Benazir Bhutto	Bilateral visit
22 Nov 1990	Male	Chandrasekhar	Nawaz Sharif	SAARC Summit
24 May 1991	New Delhi	Chandrasekhar	Nawaz Sharif	Rajiv Gandhi's funeral
17 Oct 1991	Harare	Narasimha Rao	Nawaz Sharif	CHOGM Meeting
21 Dec 1991	Colombo	Narasimha Rao	Nawaz Sharif	SAARC Summit
02 Feb 1992	Davos	Narasimha Rao	Nawaz Sharif	World Economic Forum Meeting
14 Jun 1992	Rio de Janeiro	Narasimha Rao	Nawaz Sharif	Environment Meet
03 Sep 1992	Jakarta	Narasimha Rao	Nawaz Sharif	NAM Summit
11 Apr 1992	Dhaka	Narasimha Rao	Nawaz Sharif	SAARC Summit
02 May 1995	New Delhi	Narasimha Rao	Farooq Ahmed Leghari	SAARC Summit
12 May 1997	Male	IK Gujral	Nawaz Sharif	SAARC Summit
23 Sep 1997	New York	IK Gujral	Nawaz Sharif	UN GA Meeting
25 Oct 1997	Edinburgh	IK Gujral	Nawaz Sharif	CHOGM Meeting
15 Jan 1998	Dhaka	IK Gujral	Nawaz Sharif	Indo-Pak-Bangladesh trilateral business summit
29 July 1998	Colombo	AB Vajpayee	Nawaz Sharif	SAARC Summit
29 July 1998	New York	AB Vajpayee	Nawaz Sharif	UN GA Meeting
20-21 Feb 1999	Lahore	AB Vajpayee	Nawaz Sharif	Lahore Summit
July 2001	Agra	AB Vajpayee	Pervez Musharraf	Agra Summit

Source: www.meadev.nic.in/agra-summit/chr-sum.htm.

The foreign secretary level talks were the first major attempt by the Atal Behari Vajpayee government after the nuclear tests in May 1998. They started with a joint statement issued by the foreign secretaries of India and Pakistan in September 1998, which read:

> The Foreign Secretaries will commence the substantive dialogue with separate meetings on (a) peace and security including CBMs [confidence-building measures] and (b) Jammu and Kashmir in Islamabad on 15-18 October 1998. The remaining six subjects i.e., (c) Siachen, (d) Wullar Barrage/Tulbul Navigation Project, (e) Sir Creek, (f) Terrorism and Drug Trafficking, (g) Economic and Commercial Cooperation, and (h) Promotion of friendly exchanges in various fields, shall be taken up in substantive and separate meetings in New Delhi in the first half of November 1998.[3]

Subsequently the talks on these various issues did take place during November 1998 in New Delhi. However, the talks did not succeed due to differences, invariably on all issues. Though the talks failed at the foreign secretary level, the prime ministers of India and Pakistan made another bold attempt to improve the relations between the two countries, which resulted in the Lahore summit and the subsequent declaration in February 1999.

The Lahore Declaration held that both India and Pakistan:

- shall intensify their efforts to resolve all issues, including the issue of Jammu and Kashmir.
- shall refrain from intervention and interference in each other's internal affairs.
- shall intensify their composite and integrated dialogue

3. See the text of joint statement made by the foreign secretaries of India and Pakistan, *The Hindu*, September 25, 1998.

process for an early and positive outcome of the agreed bilateral agenda.

- shall take immediate steps for reducing the risk of accidental or unauthorized use of nuclear weapons and discuss concepts and doctrines with a view to elaborating measures for confidence building in the nuclear and conventional fields, aimed at prevention of conflict.
- reaffirm their commitment to the goals and objectives of SAARC and to concert their efforts towards the realization of the SAARC vision for the year 2000 and beyond with a view to promoting the welfare of the peoples of South Asia and to improve their quality of life through accelerated economic growth, social progress and cultural development.
- reaffirm their condemnation of terrorism in all its forms and manifestations and their determination to combat this menace.
- shall promote and protect all human rights and fundamental freedoms[4]

The Lahore Declaration was seen by India as the beginning of a new era—an era in which India believed that there could be real peace and understanding with Pakistan. This was coupled with the belief that democracy had finally dawned inside Pakistan and its military was under political control. The dismissal of General Jehangir Karamat by Pakistan Prime Minister Nawaz Sharif was indicative of civilian political supremacy over the military.

---

4. See the Lahore Declaration signed between the prime ministers of India and Pakistan on February 21, 1999, available at http://www.indianembassy.org/South_Asia/Pakistan/lahoredeclaration.html.

Table 2.2: Major Agreements between India and Pakistan since the Simla Agreement

Venue and Date	Leaders of India and Pakistan	Agreements/Understandings
New Delhi, 01 Nov 1982	Indira Gandhi & Zia ul-Haq	Decision to form a Joint Commission to discuss bilateral issues Decision to continue discussions on the "mutual guarantees of non-aggression and non-use of force"[5] proposals and "Peace, Friendship and Cooperation"[6] proposals that were circulated earlier by Pakistan and India respectively
New Delhi, 10 Mar 1983	Indira Gandhi & Zia ul-Haq	Establishment of a Joint Commission to discuss various issues between India and Pakistan[7]
Islamabad, 29-31 Dec 1988	Rajiv Gandhi and Benazir Bhutto	Signing of three bilateral agreements: Prohibition of attack on each other's nuclear installations and facilities

5 Pakistan formally proposed a set of suggestions in April 1981 to India, when the conflict in Afghanistan was peaking on non-aggression and non-use of force. In June 1982, Pakistan revised the same proposal, after incorporating some suggestions from India.

6. After receiving the June 1982 non-aggression proposals of Pakistan, India formally proposed a "Treaty of Peace, Friendship and Cooperation" in August 1982, instead of a non-aggression pact.

7. The first meeting of the Joint Commission took place on June 4, 1983, in which it was decided to form sub-commissions on economic relations, information, education, travel, and tourism.

		Cultural cooperation Avoidance of double taxation on incomes derived from international civil aviation transactions
Islamabad, 16-17 July 1989	Rajiv Gandhi and Benazir Bhutto	Joint communiqué expressing the desire to work towards a comprehensive settlement to reduce the chances of conflict and promote avoidance of the use of force
Male, 21-23 Nov 1990	Chandrashekar and Nawaz Sharif	Decision to set up an additional hot line between the two leaders Decision to resume talks at foreign secretary levels[8]
Male, 12 May 1997	IK Gujral and Nawaz Sharif	Decision to reactivate the hotline Decision to constitute Joint Working Groups on various issues between India and Pakistan[9]
Lahore, 20-21 Feb 1999	AB Vajpayee and Nawaz Sharif	Lahore Declaration and Memorandum of Understanding (MoU) between the foreign secretaries of India and Pakistan

8. As a result of this meeting, the foreign secretaries met in December 1990 and agreed to evolve a "bilateral code of conduct on treatment of diplomats."
9. Joint Working Groups (JWGs) were formed to discuss Kashmir, Peace and Security, Siachen, Wular Barrage, Sir Creek, Terrorism and Drug Trafficking, Economic Cooperation, and Promotion of Friendly Ties. The talks at the JWGs level broke in September 1997, when Pakistan insisted on Kashmir as the core issue.

With the political process in tatters, the main question facing India was how to tackle Pakistan and convince its rulers that India was serious about the situation emerging inside Kashmir, without risking a conventional full-scale war? The Indian political and military leadership, drawing a leaf from their Kargil experience, advocated a similar exercise to be initiated by India on the other side of the Line of Control. Thus was born the idea of limited war with Pakistan on the heights of Kargil after India realized that the political road to Islamabad was closed.

George Fernandes was the first political leader to formally declare as early as January 2000 that there existed an option for limited war.[10] According to Fernandes, such a limited war would supplant political objectives. Explaining his concept of limited war, he observed:

> The method of employing military power has been undergoing significant changes. Use of armed forces has moved much closer to the process of diplomacy. Historically, the soldiers took over when the diplomats failed and the diplomats had to take over when the soldiers came up against a block. In more modern times, the diplomat and the soldier have to work hand in hand particularly since the application of military power can serve a rational purpose only if directed by political goals and objectives.[11]

Continuing Militancy in Kashmir

Was the failure of the political process the only reason for the evolution of limited war theory in India? For decades India

---

10. George Fernandes, while addressing the Institute of Defence Studies and Analyses (IDSA)—a leading think tank established by the government of India—spoke about the idea of limited war with Pakistan for the first time in January 2000. "Fernandes Unveils 'Limited War' Doctrine," *The Hindu*, January 25, 2000.
11. George Fernandes, "The Dynamics of Limited War," *Strategic Affairs* (October 16, 2000), http://www.stratmag.com/ issueOct-15/page07.htm.

has been living with the deadlocked process, which is based on a "one step forward two steps backward" dictum. However, it was the persistent militancy in Jammu and Kashmir that made India look for an alternative strategy.

Militancy in Jammu and Kashmir started slowly in the late 1980s, reached a peak in the early 1990s, started declining in the mid-1990s, and spiked again after the Kargil conflict, after which it steadily increased.

Table 2.3: Militancy in Jammu and Kashmir

	Militants Killed	Security Personnel Killed	Civilians Killed	Total
1988	1	1	29	31
1989	0	13	79	92
1990	183	132	862	1177
1991	614	185	594	1393
1992	873	177	859	1909
1993	1328	216	1023	2567
1994	1651	236	1012	2899
1995	1338	297	1161	2796
1996	1194	376	1333	2903
1997	1177	355	840	2372
1998	1045	339	877	2261
1999	1184	555	799	2538
2000	1808	638	842	3288
2001	2850	590	1067	4507
2002	1714	469	839	3022
2003	1546	338	658	2542

Source: South Asia Terrorism Portal, http://satp.org/satporgtp/countries/india/states/jandk/data_sheet/ annual_casualties.htm.

Counter-militancy operations apart, the Indian government also attempted to deal with the militants politically, but in vain. In 2000, the Union government attempted two ceasefires, the first one with the Hizbul Mujahideen, in July 2000 and the second one a unilateral ceasefire in December 2000.

India believed that the first ceasefire failed due to Pakistan's pressure on the Hizbul Mujahideen. It all started with Majid Dar, who was later killed by his own group, announcing a unilateral cease-fire on July 24, 2000 in Srinagar. The statement read:

> The primary objective of the announcement is to break the deadlock and make the atmosphere conducive for talks...There is a craving worldwide that peace and normality should return to the subcontinent which is passing through difficult times. Our decision is also in consonance with the statements by the Hurriyat leaders and the popular feelings...If India accepted our proposal and expressed its willingness for a meaningful dialogue it will be extended...[12]

At that point in time, the Hizbul Mujahideen was undivided, and its supreme leader Syed Salahuddin endorsed the call for the ceasefire.[13] The Union government and the Hizbul announced their team for dialogues on July 28 and 30 respectively. Just a day before the scheduled meeting between the representatives of the government and Hizbul, Salahuddin suddenly announced that if the Indian government did not include Pakistan in the negotiations by August 8, 2000, the

---

12. "Hizbul Announces Cease-fire," *The Hindu*, July 25, 2000.
13. Salahuddin was quoted as saying, "We own this offer, it is a tactical move...We have thrown the ball in India's court. It must now respond positively." See "Hizbul Chied Endorses Ceasefire," *Hindustan Times*, July 26, 2000.

Hizbul would rethink the ceasefire offer.[14] India refused to include anyone else in its dialogue with the Hizbul.[15] On August 8, the Hizbul announced that it withdrew the ceasefire and resumed hostilities.[16] The Indian government blamed Pakistan for pressurizing the Hizbul to include a rider to the ceasefire offer and later to withdraw it.[17]

The second ill-fated ceasefire of 2000 was initiated as a unilateral announcement from the Union government on November 19, 2000. It too failed, as there were no takers for the government initiative. For its part, the government did not have clear objectives and failed to plan any corresponding dialogues with the ceasefire offer. It only requested local participation by those in Kashmir, six months after the announcement of the ceasefire, to discuss "peace and how it may be attained."[18] K.C. Pant was appointed as the interlocutor to initiate a dialogue in Kashmir. Due to various factors, the Pant mission failed to take off.

The continuing militancy and the failure to curb it completely, either through political or military means thus was another reason that made India realize that it could not control it unless cross-border aspects of militancy were contained.

How to combat militancy when militants are being trained, provided safe havens, and drawing material support from across the border? India expected the international community, especially the United States, to pressure Pakistan from supporting cross-border militancy, but all its efforts proved unsuccessful.

---

14. "Salahuddin Sets August 8 as Deadline for Tripartite Talks," *The Hindu*, August 4, 2000.
15. "No Role for Pakistan: PM," *The Hindu*, August 7, 2000.
16. "Hizbul Mujahideen Revokes Ceasefire," *The Hindu*, August 9, 2000.
17. "Govt. Blames Pak., Open for Talks," *The Hindu*, August 9, 2000.
18. "Centre Invites Militants, Hurriyat for Dialogue on Kashmir," *The Daily Excelsior*, April 6, 2000.

Unable to prevent militancy in Kashmir politically and militarily and not in a position to bring about international pressure on Pakistan to give up its support for cross-border terrorism, India started looking for a new strategy to deal with the problem on its own. Surgical strikes of militant camps and hot pursuit of militants across the Line of Control (LoC) were considered as two main strategies that India could rely upon while combating cross-border terrorism.

Inherent in the strategies of hot pursuit and surgical strikes are the dangers of escalation. What if Pakistan decides to escalate the conflict during or after a hot pursuit? To be prepared to face the military consequences of the escalation, India needed an overall strategy, with which it could carry out operations against the militants on the other side of the LoC, without risking a large-scale conflict. The strategy of limited war fit India's requirement of pursuing its immediate military strategies to combat militancy, yet without escalating the conflict level.

Kargil as a Limited Conflict

More than the failure at military and political levels to deal with the militancy, the military operations in Kargil made India believe that, like Pakistan, India could also carry out a military operation across the LoC. An extended analysis of the Kargil conflict is essential, since India's concept of limited war is largely based on what happened in May and June of 1999 both in Kargil and outside it.

The conflict in Kargil started with three shepherds observing movement of irregular and regular troops from the other side of the LoC on May 3, 1999, on the Jubbar Heights of Kargil sector.[19] The intrusions were reported to the local Punjab

19. Initially there was a controversy over the composition of the infiltrators. India, right from the beginning has been accusing Pakistan of sending its

regiment, which had sent two patrols to investigate into the intrusions on May 4 and 5. Two more patrols were sent on May 7 and one more on May 14, 1999. Though the Indian army was convinced that Pakistan's support for militancy would continue irrespective of the Lahore summit and the subsequent declaration, it never expected such a large-scale organized operation from the Pakistani side.[20] Even the Kargil Review Committee, which was constituted later to examine the war, concluded that the intrusions came as a surprise.

Until May 14, 1999, there was no report in the media about what was happening in the Kargil sector. Most of the reports between May 10 and 13 focused on "heavy shelling."[21] On May 10, reports mentioned about "eight to ten artillery shells" hitting the "cantonment base at Kargil" and "troops as well as civilians" being evacuated from there.[22] On May 11 it was reported that the "Pakistani troops fired around 70 artillery shells," from which no military personnel suffered any damage, except for a coolie working with the Indian army who was killed, and three civilians who were injured.[23] The same report also mentioned most people from Baroo village and Kargil

---

regular troops along with the *mujahideen*. Pakistan, though, refused to acknowledge the presence of any regular troops initially. However, their presence has been proved beyond a doubt and even accepted by writers from Pakistan at a later stage.

20. One day before the shepherds identified intrusion in Kargil, General V.P. Malik made an interesting and perceptive observation. He said on May 2, 1999, "It is in our assessment that Pakistan will continue to pursue belligerence, abet infiltration and indulge in proxy war at a higher level. The recent Lahore Declaration has not in any way changed the ground situation in Kashmir. If anything, the Pakistani Army and ISI [Inter Services Intelligence] are still active in aiding and abetting terrorism in the state." See "Malik Sees Trouble on Pak Front," *The Times of India*, May 3, 1999 .
21. "Kargil Shelled Again by Pak Rangers," *The Hindu*, May 10, 1999.
22. "Arms Dump Blown up in Shelling in Kargil," *Daily Excelsior*, May 10, 1999.

town migrating "to safer places in view of increasing threat to their life and property in the exchange of shelling."[24]

The enormity of the intrusion was reported for the first time in regional newspapers in Kashmir. *The Daily Excelsior* on May 12, 1999 reported that in the early morning of May 11, "An Army patrol spotted a group of 200 to 300 foreign militants which seemed to have infiltrated into this side for the last three days. Almost the entire brigade strength of 121-Infantry was immediately mobilized for what could possibly be the largest counter-insurgency operation of the last 10 years in Jammu & Kashmir." For the first time, the firing along the LoC by the Pakistani troops for the previous three days was seen as an effort by Pakistan to provide cover for the infiltrators.[25] The local media reported on May 13, 1999 about "heavy casualties" near the LoC at Kargil as a result of a "fierce battle" between "Indian security forces and a thick group of Pakistani infiltrators." The same report also mentioned about two companies of paratroopers being airlifted from Kupwara and "dropped at strategically important points in Kargil border area."[26] For the first time, reports were made on infiltrators capturing posts two to five kilometers inside the Indian side of the LoC. The one-line official response for these developments was that "the Defence authorities neither confirm nor deny the report."[27]

On May 13, the Jammu correspondent of Doordarshan

---

23. "Coolie Killed, Three Injured in Kargil Shelling," *Daily Excelsior*, May 11, 1999.
24. Ibid.
25. "LoC Turns into Battlefield: 200 Pakistani Militants Storm into Kargil," *Daily Excelsior*, May 12, 1999.
26. "Heavy Casualties Feared in Kargil Operation: Hospital, Civilian Population Evacuated," *Daily Excelsior*, May 13, 1999.
27. The LoC in this sector was also believed to have been captured by the infiltrators before they moved two to five kilometers into this side of the border.

reported Lt. Col. S.P.K. Singh, the Public Relations Officer of Northern Command Headquarters, as confirming the death of seven Indian soldiers and ten militants. For the first time, it was reported in the regional press that the Indian army authorities at Kargil had begun to believe that it was actually Pakistani regular army personnel who had made the incursion on Tuesday, captured two Indian posts and killed a group of four Indian soldiers. Officials have now developed doubts regarding the identity of the intruders who had earlier been described as "Pakhtoon-like militants."[28]

Yet there was no mention about such intrusions in the national media. *The Hindu* reported on May 14, 1999 of a "war-like situation in Kargil," in which the "the presence of scores of militants with the Army" was not ruled out.[29] *The Hindu* reported on May 15 that the Defence Ministry denied "reports about the fall of an Indian post at the wake of Pakistani firing in Kargil." However, the Defence Ministry was quoted as saying that "Pakistani Army regulars and trained Mujahideens had infiltrated the area under the cover of fire." Infiltrators were then believed to have "occupied some remote and 'unheld' areas" and that "further inflow of militants in the area had been stopped."[30] On May 19, 1999, it was reported that the Indian army had "gunned down 52 heavily armed Pakistan-backed militants and injured many others" and in the process lost nine men. It was reported that "an estimated 350 militants, dressed like local shepherds, had been pushed in by Pakistan Army under the cover of artillery gunfire."[31]

Irrespective of visits by the defense minister and the chief

28. "Pak Troops Believed Engaged in Battle: Army Confirms Seventeen Casualties in Kargil," *Daily Excelsior*, May 14, 1999.
29. "War-like Situation in Kargil," *The Hindu*, May 14, 1999.
30. "Indian Posts Safe: Defence Ministry," *The Hindu*, May 15, 1999.
31. "52 Militants Died in Kargil Operation," *The Indian Express*, May 19, 1999.

of army staff, India did not yet realize the extent of infiltration.[32] George Fernandes mentioned on May 14 that there was no need to be worried about the sporadic shelling by Pakistan[33] and on May 16 announced that the infiltrators from the Kargil sector would be pushed out in forty-eight hours.[34]

On May 22, Farooq Abdullah, the chief minister of Jammu and Kashmir, presided over a meeting of the Unified Headquarters in Jammu, which was also attended by the chief secretary; Mr. Ashok Jaitly, security advisor to the state government; Lt. General A.S. Khanna, General Officer Commanding (GOC) 16 Corps; Director General Police, Mr. Gurbachan Jagat; and Principal Secretary, Home, Mr. C. Phunsog. The focus was rather on the militant situation on Jammu, especially the anti-militancy operations in the Doda, Udhampur, Poonch, and Rajouri districts. The meeting was said to have discussed various issues including "supply of water, electricity, civic amenities, shifting of Jammu Bus Stand, installation of street lights, local bodies, cement shortage and transport hazards."[35] On May 23, Maj. Gen. P.P.S. Bindera at the Northern Command HQ was quoted as claiming that the infiltrators were on the run in the Drass and Batalik sectors, since they had exhausted their ammunition and their firepower was reduced drastically.[36]

During this first phase, India deliberately wanted to downplay the events as a mere localized flare-up. Lt. General

---

32. Defence Minister George Fernandes visited the Kargil sector on May 13, 1999 (*Daily Excelsior*, May 14, 1999). Gen. Malik visited the areas on May 23 (*Hindustan Times*, May 24, 1999).
33. "Forces Well Prepared: George," *Daily Excelsior*, May 15, 1999.
34. "Infiltration Will Be Pushed out in 48 Hours: George," *Daily Excelsior*, May 17, 1999.
35. "Unified Hqrs Review Security Situation," *Daily Excelsior*, May 22, 1999.
36. "Ammunition over, Infiltrators on the Run, Claims Army," *The Indian Express*, May 24, 1999.

Krishan Pal, GOC, 15 Corps felt that Pakistan was "itching for a limited war but we will not fall into this trap."[37]

May 25 was a crucial day in the conflict. For the first time, it was stated by the Indian military leadership that eviction would be a tougher job and that no conclusive timeframe to end the operation could be foreseen. Maj. Gen. J. J. Singh, Additional Director, Military Operations was quoted as telling that the infiltrators had taken up positions up to six kilometers inside Indian territory and were spread over large areas in Drass, Batalik, Kaksar, and Mashkoh.[38] He also observed that the infiltrators possessed sophisticated instruments including missiles, radars, snowmobiles, mortars, sophisticated military communication equipment, and automatic weapons.[39] Thus for the first time, the military came to realize and publicly acknowledge the extent of the infiltration, the weapons that the infiltrators possessed, and the possible time that it would take to evict them.

May 25 was also important as the date of the first meeting of the Cabinet Committee on Security (CCS) to review the situation, three weeks after the infiltrators were spotted for the first time on May 3. This meeting ended the initial phase of Indian ignorance on the extent of infiltration and also signified the Indian resolve to fight infiltration, both militarily and politically.

Surprisingly, not long before India held its first major meeting on the infiltration, Nawaz Sharif, the prime minister of Pakistan, had a meeting with General Pervez Musharraf on May 22 and decided "to give a befitting response to India, if

---

37. Quoted in Ramesh Vinayak, "Nasty Surprise," *India Today* (May 31, 1999): 21.
38. "Eviction Difficult, Admits Army," *The Times of India*, May 26, 1999.
39. Ibid.

New Delhi launched any misadventure at the Line of Control."[40] On the same day that India called its first CCS meeting, Pakistan also had a meeting at a comparable level, attended by its political and military leadership.[41]

On the military front, the Indian Air Force (IAF) was put into action beginning on May 26, which signaled the beginning of the second phase. It was a clear indication that India was ready to escalate the conflict to protect its interests. The official statement mentioned, "This is the start of the operations and they would continue till our defence forces re-occupy our territory...Any escalation of this conflict will be entirely the responsibility of Pakistan."[42] Though Pakistan threatened that it would retaliate, India continued with the aerial bombings.[43] At the same time, India also decided to establish hotline contact at the Director General of Military Operations (DGMO) level with Pakistan.[44] At a political level, Vajpayee contacted Nawaz Sharif and told him that India would not allow any intrusion to take place on its territory.[45] George Fernandes met the heads of the US and UK missions in New Delhi and apprised them of the latest developments.[46] The military operations took more

---

40. "PM, COAS Discuss Indian Build-up at LoC," *The News*, May 23, 1999.
41. The high-level meeting took place in Islamabad on May 25 and was attended by the foreign minister, Kashmir affairs minister, defense secretary, acting army chief, director general military operations (DGMO), and commander of 10 Corps. *The News*, May 26, 1999.
42. "IAF Bombs Militant Posts," *The Hindu*, May 27, 1999.
43. Sartaj Aziz, the then foreign minister of Pakistan, responded to the use of the Indian air force by stating, "We are retaliating and we will retaliate." "Indian Action Unwarranted, Says Pak," *The Hindu*, May 27, 1999.
44. "Armies Establish Contact on Hotline," *The Times of India*, May 27, 1999.
45. In a meeting at Pondicherry on May 25, 1999, Vajpayee stated: "In my talks with Pakistan Prime Minister yesterday, I had made it clear that we will not allow any intrusion to take place in our territory. We will clear our territory." "PM Speaks to Sharif, Says India Won't Allow Infiltration," *Daily Excelsior*, May 26, 1999.
46. "George Meets Oppn Leaders, Heads of US, UK Missions," *The Indian Express*, May 27, 1999.

than two weeks to reach any positive results at the ground level. The first major achievement was the recapture of Batalik Top on June 11, 1999.

The period between May 26 and June 10 could be called the second phase of the conflict, in which India began its effort in earnest to defend its territory. This phase was a defensive one, as it tried with great difficulty— given the terrain and logistical problems—to drive the infiltrators away. This phase witnessed several events that threatened to escalate and at the same time also stabilized and limited the conflict. The threats to escalate the conflict came primarily from Pakistan.

First was Pakistan's military response. On May 27, 1999, Pakistan shot down an Indian MiG-21 aircraft, killing Sqn. Ldr. Ojha. Another pilot, Flt. Lt. Nachiketa, was captured as he ejected from his MiG-27 after it experienced a mechanical problem. On May 28, the infiltrators shot down a Mi-17 helicopter on the Indian side of the LoC.

Second was Pakistan's threat to escalate the conflict. On May 27, Nawaz Sharif was quoted as saying that the nuclear tests of 1998 had provided Pakistan the confidence to counter any attack. He was further quoted as pronouncing that the people of Pakistan "are confident for the first time in their history that in the eventuality of an armed attack they will be able to meet it on equal terms." Clearly, Sharif was indicating the military failure of the previous wars with India was no longer in their minds, as the nuclear tests had given them new confidence. On May 31, Pakistan Foreign Secretary Shamsad Ahmad explicitly warned: "We [Pakistan] will not hesitate to use any weapon in our arsenal to defend our territorial integrity."

Third was the failure to communicate to each other at the highest political level. Vajpayee and Nawaz Sharif had signed the Lahore Declaration only months before. More importantly, Vajpayee and Sharif had decided to engage in secret negotiations after the summit in Lahore. R.K. Mishra, a respected Indian politician and journalist, and Niaz A. Naik, former foreign secretary of Pakistan, were chosen as the trusted emissaries of Vajpayee and Sharif and were holding secret parleys in New Delhi and Islamabad.[47] Before the conflict reached its climax in Kargil, there were six rounds of talks between March 3 and May 17, 1999.[48] There were specific questions from the Indian side to Pakistan on the meetings of April 12, April 21, and May 17, 1999. To quote Niaz Naik:

> On 12 April...Mishra came again to Islamabad. This time, however, he appeared to be a little perturbed. Vajpayee had told him that Indian intelligence was reporting that the usual springtime infiltration of militants across the LOC was already underway. *Nawaz Sharif told Mishra in my presence that he would use his influence to correct the situation.*[49]

---

47. Niaz Naik has explained the substance of the talks between the two emissaries later in many of his exclusive interviews on the subject. R.K. Mishra to date has not spoken about the Indian perspective of the secret negotiations that he had with Naik. Robert G. Wirsing has given a detailed account of Naik's views in his recent book on Kashmir. See Robert G. Wirsing, *Kashmir in the Shadow of War: Regional Rivalries in a Nuclear Age* (Armonk, NY: M.E. Sharpe, 2003): 25-33. See also Kushanava Choudhury, "After the Lahore Summit: The Real Story," http://www.rediff.com/news/2000/nov/23naik.htm. For Indian, Pakistani, and international analyses of the talks see A.G. Noorani, "An Aborted Deal," *Frontline* 16, no. 18 (September 10, 1999); Suzanne Goldenberg, "Early Deal to End Kashmir Conflict Was Ignored," *The Guardian*, July 22, 1999.
48. The first round actually took place between R.K. Mishra and Anwar Zahid during March 3 and 4 in Islamabad. After the sudden demise of Zahid, Mishra met Naik in Islamabad on March 20. The third round was in New Delhi between March 27 and April 1, 1999; the fourth round in Islamabad on April 12; the fifth round in Islamabad on April 21; and the sixth round was in Islamabad on May 17. The next round of talks was to take place only on June 25, 1999 at Islamabad. See Wirsing, *Kashmir in the Shadow of War*, 25-33.
49. Wirsing, *Kashmir in the Shadow of War*, 29. Emphasis added.

On April 21, Niaz Naik continues:

> Mishra returned to Islamabad for yet another round of talks. He stated that India was now in possession of much more information about militants' infiltration across the LOC. He made no specific mention of the Kargil sector, however. *At this, Nawaz Sharif promised to take concrete steps to rectify the problem.*[50]

The May 17 meeting was significant. According to Naik:

> He [R.K. Mishra] told me that Vajpayee was under fire from hawkish elements in India. The Indian Prime Minister was still awaiting clarification of the situation from Nawaz. At this 17 May meeting…[Mishra] met with Nawaz alone while I waited outside the Prime Minister's office. There was a little tension in the air. After about ten minutes, Mishra stepped out of the Prime Minister's office to go to the washroom. In his absence, Nawaz asked me (in Punjabi): "What's wrong with him? He is asking me whether on 20 February (the date of Lahore Summit) I knew of the Kargil plan." Nawaz did not give a reply to his question, at least not in my presence. Using ambiguous language, he told Mishra that he would look into the matter.[51]

Irrespective of these three meetings, especially the last, the political leadership in India and Pakistan failed to communicate with each other on the gravity of the situation even after developing a rapport at the Lahore summit and establishing secret negotiations. Sharif, though informed by Mishra at least thrice, failed to give a satisfactory reply to Vajpayee's concerns. The third meeting was significant, as Mishra had communicated to Sharif regarding Vajpayee's doubts over his sincerity at Lahore. Sharif, after realizing that an element of mistrust was developing, could have dispatched Naik immediately to New Delhi to meet with Vajpayee either alone or with Mishra. Unfortunately that never happened, as the next meeting was scheduled only on June 25, 1999.

50. Ibid., 30. Emphasis added.
51. Ibid.

The same period also witnessed efforts by India and Pakistan at stabilizing the situation. On May 28, Nawaz Sharif announced that Pakistan was willing to send its foreign minister, Sartaj Aziz, to India to defuse the situation.[52] On June 3, Flt. Lt. Nachiketa was released and handed over to the Indian High Commissioner in Pakistan. Meanwhile the DGMOs between India and Pakistan established their hotline.[53]

Externally, there was pressure from the West, especially from the United States, to defuse the crisis. US President Bill Clinton wrote to Sharif asking him to "take steps to defuse the crisis and respect the Line of Control."

The third phase of the conflict can be traced (with slight chronological overlap with the second) from May 11 to July 5, 1999. From the recapture of the Batalik Top, the first major military achievement of this phase on May 11, India went full throttle at both military and political levels to clear the infiltrators from the Kargil sector.[54]

On the military front, India captured the crucial Tololing peak in Dras sector on June 13. The Indian military response intensified on June 17 when India launched Mirage 2000 planes to bombard the enemy supply lines in Batalik sector. The use of air power, though debated in terms of its utility in Kargil, without any doubt broke the infiltrators both physically and

---

52. "Nawaz Offers to Send Sartaj Aziz to New Delhi," *The News*, May 29, 1999.
53. "Armies Establish Contact on Hotline," *The Times of India*, May 27, 1999. While reports in India state that the hotlines were established subsequent to the telephone conversation between the two prime ministers on May 25, 1999 to discuss developments in Kargil, Pakistan perceived it differently. Pakistan saw it as a part of their weekly contact (the hotlines between the DGMOs had been functional long before the conflict, and it had been agreed that they would contact each other every week on Tuesdays) and Qureshi even complained that during the contact on May 26, the Indian DGMO did not inform his Pakistani counterpart about the air strikes. See Shakil Shaikh, "India Uses Weapons Akin to Nerve Gas Bombs," *The News*, May 27, 1999.
54. "Indian Troops Recapture Batalik Top," *The Indian Express*, May 12, 1999.

psychologically, as well as interdicting their supply lines.[55] Towards the end of June, the IAF also began night operations.[56]

Point 5140 was re-captured on June 20;[57] Point 5203 in the Batalik sector on June 21; six more heights around Point 5203 on June 23;[58] major peaks closer to the Tiger Hill on June 30; two heights on Jubar Hills on July 1; and the strategic Tiger Hill on July 5. In addition, India decided to provide an emergency allocation of Rs. 600 crore to the army to buy ammunition for its Bofors 155 MM gun.[59] The finance minister also announced that the Indian economy was capable of managing the impact of the Kargil conflict.[60]

On the political front, Vajpayee informed Clinton of India's resolve to rid its territory of the infiltrators in a telephone conversation with him on June 14. On June 15, India refused a US suggestion for diffusing the situation through direct Indo-Pak talks, stating that there could be no meaningful dialogue until the infiltrators moved back across the LoC.

India, on the bilateral front, refused to negotiate with

---

55. See the following news reports for discussion of the effectiveness of the air power. "IAF Hits Enemy Supply Base," *The Hindu*, June 18, 1999; "IAF Jets Pound Tiger Hills," *The Hindu*, June 25, 1999; "IAF Pounding of Enemy on Top of Tiger Hill Continues," *Hindustan Times*, June 26, 1999; "IAF Strikes Supply Base in Batalik," *The Hindu*, June 27, 1999; "IAF Laser Bombs Zero in on Camps," *The Asian Age*, June 27, 1999.
56. According to an IAF spokesperson, "Night operations will create fear and uncertainty and wear the intruders down. We want to deny them even a good night's sleep." See "IAF Begins Round-the-clock Operations against Intruders," *The Hindu*, June 28, 1999.
57. "Army Recaptures Point 5140," *The Pioneer*, June 21, 1999.
58. "Troops Capture 6 More Heights," *The Pioneer*, June 24, 1999.
59. "Rs 600 Crore More for Defence," *The Times of India*, June 14, 1999.
60. Yashwant Sinha, the then finance minister of India, was quoted as saying, "Since the economic fundamentals are strong and there are early signs of a revival, any possible impact of the Kargil conflict is very manageable." "Economy Robust Enough to Bear Kargil Cost: FM," *Hindustan Times*, June 15, 1999.

Pakistan, except on the question of Pakistan withdrawing from the Kargil heights. On June 1, Fernandes announced: "There is no question of negotiating any ceasefire: our position is very clear. All those who have been pushed into our territory by the Pakistani side, including Pakistani troops, should go back."[61] When Pakistan volunteered to send Foreign Minister Sartaj Aziz to India for talks in the first week of June, India showed its reluctance by telling Pakistan that the date was not convenient for it to do so.[62] The Foreign Office spokesman of India, responding to Aziz's earlier statement that the LoC is not well defined, retorted, "The Line of Control is well defined and fully settled. We would like to make it clear that the comments relating to the LoC made by the Pakistani Foreign Minister cannot be the subject for discussion."[63] When Aziz finally came to New Delhi on June 12, 1999 and met Foreign Minister Jaswant Singh, the latter gave him two points—to vacate the aggression in Kargil and to restore the status quo ante—while the former wanted to have a wide discussion. Responding to a question, Jaswant Singh stressed that the meeting that he had with Aziz was not a part of any dialogue. He was quoted as saying that "it will be a misnomer to call it a dialogue" and "the dialogue process was abandoned by Pakistan through misadventure."[64]

---

61. "Cease-fire Only after Infiltrators Quit: Fernandes," *The Hindu*, June 2, 1999.
62. "June 7 'Not Convenient' for Talks," *The Hindu*, June 6, 1999. Sartaj Aziz could only respond that "For Pakistan, there was no constraint, but we need to hear from them [the Indians] about the visit...We are ready to hold talks any time." See "Pak Ready for Talks Any Time: Sartaj Aziz," *The Asian Age*, June 8, 1999.
63. "LoC Is 'Fully' Settled," *The Hindu*, June 5, 1999. Tariq Altaf, Pakistan's spokesman of the foreign ministry later explained what Aziz meant: "The line is drawn on the map. There is no demarcation on the ground. No wire or posts or signs for LoC and that is why India violates it time and again." See "Indian on 'Warpath', Accuses Pakistan," *The Times of India*, June 8, 1999.

The next bilateral move, which was held secretly, was to reactivate the Mishra-Naik track. After the previous meeting on May 17, R.K. Mishra went to Islamabad on June 25 and met Niaz Naik. There are several accounts of Mishra's trip to Islamabad. A.G. Noorani, a highly respected commentator in India, wrote that the meeting took place much earlier. According to him, Mishra traveled with Vivek Katju on June 18.[65] According to Nazim Zehra, a Pakistani journalist, both Mishra and Katju reached Islamabad on June 20, 1999 to meet Sharif.[66] According to Niaz Naik, however, Mishra told Naik on June 25 that India and Pakistan were "one inch away from war" and asked Naik to convey that to Sharif.[67] On receiving the message from Mishra, according to Niaz Naik, Sharif prepared a written message for Vajpayee consisting of the following four points:

- Both prime ministers should reiterate their commitment to the Lahore process;
- Both India and Pakistan should take concrete steps to restore the sanctity of the Line of Control;
- The Indian side should stop the shelling and aerial bombing in the Kargil sector in order to restore an atmosphere conducive to peace, and
- Both prime ministers should renew efforts to complete the process started at Lahore to include resolution of all issues between them, including Jammu and Kashmir.[68]

Naik went to New Delhi on Vajpayee's invitation and met with him on June 27 to discuss the four points. Vajpayee told him:

---

64. K.K. Katyal, "Stalemate in Indo-Pak. Talks," *The Hindu*, June 13, 1999.
65. A.G. Noorani, "Kargil Diplomacy," *Frontline* 16, no. 16 (August 13, 1999).
66. Nasim Zehra, "Covert Contacts," *The News*, July 2, 1999.
67. Wirsing, *Kashmir in the Shadow of War*, 30.

> Pakistan should announce the withdrawal of its forces from Kargil and all would be ok. I [Niaz Naik] stressed that *both* sides would have to commit themselves to withdrawal. Vajpayee repeated that the directors-general of military operations of each side's army should together work out a plan for the mutual withdrawal of forces.[69]

According to Niaz Naik, it was agreed that Nawaz Sharif would stop at New Delhi on his way to China. The plan was for Sharif to send a message of "peace and good will" to the Indian prime minister on his way to Beijing; the Indian prime minister would invite him to New Delhi. While Niaz Naik has not elaborated on what the two prime ministers planned to do in New Delhi, Nasim Zehra wrote that they hoped to sign a slightly modified four points agreement. According to Zehra the four points were:[70]

- Appropriate steps to be taken by both sides to mutually respect the LoC determined under the Simla agreement
- Immediate resumption of the composite dialogue initiated under the Lahore process
- Islamabad to use its influence on the *mujahideen* to request them to disengage
- Find an expeditious solution to the Kashmir dispute within the specified time-frame

Information on the meeting leaked and the meeting did not materialize. According to Naik and Zehra, India backtracked and instead of agreeing to invite Sharif to New Delhi, Vajpayee issued a warning that "Pakistan must withdraw its forces from Kargil or New Delhi would take appropriate action."[71]

68. Ibid., 30-31.
69. Ibid., 31.
70. Nasim Zehra, *The News*, July 27, 1998. The same has also been quoted in Amit Baruah, "The Plan That Failed," *The Hindu*, July 28, 1999.
71. Wirsing, *Kashmir in the Shadow of War*, 32.

Why did New Delhi fail to go ahead with the meeting and Vajpayee refuse to sign such an agreement? According to Noorani, "Had the deal gone through on June 27, the result would have been vastly better than the one that came after July 11. Bilateralism would have received a powerful boost."[72] In fact, without knowing that both were so close to signing an agreement, there was an element of support for the Naik-Mishra diplomacy.[73] Many inside India were hopeful of a peaceful settlement with Pakistan, but it was not meant to be.[74] The reason, according to Noorani, was that "some people in New Delhi wanted to flourish a military victory for electoral ends, in preference to a diplomatic situation."[75]

India deliberately downplayed and ignored the war

---

72. Noorani, "Kargil Diplomacy."
73. Without knowing that it was a joint effort, *Indian Express* in its editorial commented that there was no reason for the Vajpayee government to sound defensive to the Naik initiative. See "Back-channel Diplomacy," *The Indian Express*, July 1, 1999. Yet another editorial also claimed "there is nothing intrinsically wrong about Mr Vajpayee's two-track approach—firmness on the ground and maintenance of open channels for a mutually acceptable settlement." See "Nation Must Know," *Hindustan Times*, July 2, 1999.
74. There were many critics who believed that Sharif could not be trusted. In retrospect, it is clear now that Sharif's role in Kargil was limited and that the Pakistani army planned the incursions. However, at that time there were not many who were willing to believe that. Asking, "What prompts us [India] to believe Nawaz Sharif," M.J. Akbar argues, "The new ceasefire line could become Tiger hills, if Mr Vajpayee is too earnest about peace. Pakistan created a military problem. India has only one solution: a military solution." M.J. Akbar, "Nawaz Sharif's Second Peace Trap," *The Asian Age*, July 4, 1999. Muchkund Dubey, India's former foreign secretary, wrote, "What we need are military gains. This will determine our ability to guard our borders in that area in future and better equip us to withstand the pressure...Diplomacy must take the back stage as the situation in Kargil is too complex, sensitive and difficult to be managed by diplomatic devices." See Muchkund Dubey, "Kargil & the Limits of Diplomacy," *The Hindu*, July 5, 1999. *The Pioneer*, in its editorial, noted, "There can be no ceasefire agreement till the last intruder has vacated Indian territory, alive or dead, preferably the latter." See "Win the Peace," *The Pioneer*, July 6, 1999.
75. Noorani, "Kargil Diplomacy."

threats from Pakistan during this period.[76] Vajpayee made a symbolic tour to Kashmir during the second week of June and reiterated once again that talks with Pakistan were possible only after the latter pulled back its troops from Kargil.[77] To Sharif's threat issued on June 20 to have "more Kargil-like situations,"[78] India issued a counter threat on June 23; at a press conference, Gen. V.P. Malik made a deliberate statement: "If necessary, we [Indian troops] can cross the LoC in the supreme national interest, but the decision lies with the cabinet."[79]

The last phase of the conflict started from July 5—the day on which Sharif signed an agreement with Clinton agreeing to respect the Line of Control. The statement read: It was agreed between the President [of the United States] and Prime Minister [of Pakistan] that concrete steps will be taken for the restoration of the Line of Control in accordance with the Simla agreement.[80]

Though there was a lot of opposition from inside Pakistan against the Clinton-Sharif agreement, the government at Islamabad initiated measures to de-escalate the conflict. The Indian army continued its operations against the infiltrators, as the infiltrators did not leave and continued fighting. Point 4812 and Dog Hill were recaptured on July 6; Jubar height and Point 4268, the next day.[81] The army cleared the infiltrators and reached the LoC on Batalik sector on July 9;[82] Rocky Knob,

---

76. A Pakistani official said, "When diplomacy fails, war becomes inevitable." "War Inevitable if Diplomacy Fails, Warns Pakistan," *The Times of India*, June 15, 1999.
77. "Withdraw Troops, PM Tells Pak.," *The Hindu*, June 15, 1999.
78. Sharif stated "Kargil is an aspect of Kashmir issue...If the Kashmir issue is not resolved once and for all according to the wishes of Kashmiri people, many more Kargil-like issues can crop up." "Sharif Warns of More Kargil-like Situations," *The Times of India*, June 21, 1999.
79. "We Can Cross the LoC, if Needed," *The Hindu*, June 24, 1999.
80. See the text of the Clinton-Sharif statement, *The Hindu*, July 6, 1999.
81. "Jubar Height Recaptured," *The Hindu*, July 8, 1999.
82. "Army Reaches LoC in Batalik," *The Hindu*, July 10, 1999.

the last major peak in Mushkoh valley, was cleared on July 10.[83] Lt. Gen. N.C. Vij, the Director General of Military Operations (DGMO), declared on July 26 that the territory was completely free from the infiltrators.[84]

Was Kargil a Limited War?

Surprisingly, the term "limited war" to describe the Kargil conflict appeared in the Pakistani media long before Indian papers and analysts started realizing the nature and intensity of the operations. A news report read, "*Pakistan Army claimed* having captured 20 Indian posts in *'limited war'* with India which involved use of missiles."[85]

In retrospect, India perceives Kargil as a limited war. Did Pakistan perceive it as a limited war, before initiating it? If the above-mentioned report is to be believed, then someone from the army should have briefed the reporter on the nature of the conflict and its progress.

The Territory

The confrontation took place in four sub-sectors—Mushkoh, Drass, Kaksar, and Batalik—covering a distance of 150 km. These sectors cover the towns of Turtok, Batalik, Kargil, Kaksar, and Dras along with the Chorbatla and Mushkoh valleys.[86]

India deliberately decided to fight within the LoC, though occasionally threats were issued about crossing over. One reason why India did not to cross the LoC was to retain

83. "Army Recovers Last Major Peak," *The Indian Express*, July 11, 1999.
84. "Eviction of Intruders Complete: DGMO," *The Hindu*, July 27, 1999.
85. "Pakistan Army Captures 20 Indian Posts," *The News*, May 17, 1999. Emphasis added.
86. For a brief analysis of these terrains see Maj. Gen. Ashok Krishna, "The Kargil War," in *Kargil: The Tables Turned*, eds. Maj. Gen. Ashok Krishna and P.R. Chari, (New Delhi: Manohar Publishers, 2001): 88-95.

international pressure on Pakistan. By not crossing the LoC, India was able to convince the international community that the conflict was initiated by Pakistan and therefore had to be diffused by the latter. There was open support for India's stand. Second, India did not want to escalate the conflict by crossing over. Irrespective of pressure within, the Indian political leadership did not want to cross the LoC, as could be seen from the statement made by Indian Air Chief Marshal Tipnis: "The government wants to ensure there is no escalation. The implications of restricted use of air power were made clear to it."[87]

The Use of Weapons

The use of weapons was limited to mortars, multi-barrel rockets, and howitzers from the Indian side. The Indian military used 300 pieces of artillery, including 100 Bofors 155 mm guns, firing an average 5,000 shells a day.[88] The infiltrators from the Pakistani side mainly used machine guns, mortars, and even surface-to-air missiles (SAMs), while Pakistani army regulars used howitzers from across the border to bombard the Indian side.

Occasionally, Pakistan used its helicopters, operating clandestinely over Indian air space.[89] It also used its Anza missiles, one of which hit the Indian MiG-21, killing its pilot Sqn. Ldr. Ojha.[90]

The infiltrators used the SAMs for the first time in the history of militancy in Kashmir.[91] It was believed that the SAMs

87. Quoted in Harinder Baweja, "Slow, but Steady," *India Today* 24, no. 26 (June 28, 1999): 21.
88. "The Action Theatre," *India Today* 24, no. 30 (July 26, 1999): 20.
89. Tipnis was quoted as saying, "Their [Pakistan's] helicopters are operating clandestinely." See Baweja, "Slow, but Steady," 17.
90. "Anza Missiles Used to Down Indian Jets," *The News*, May 28, 1999.91. Manoj Joshi and Harinder Baweja, "Blasting Peace," *India Today* 24, no. 23 (June 7, 1999): 17.

were Stinger missiles provided by the US Central Intelligence Agency (CIA) to the Afghan *mujahideen* during their fight against the Soviet Union in the 1980s.[92] The fact that the infiltrators were armed with SAMs was a clear indication that Pakistan expected India to use its air force.

The Use of Air Power

The use of air power during the conflict was also limited. Initially the Cabinet Committee on Security (CCS) of India rejected the use of the Indian Air Force as requested by its army. Both the CCS and the Air Force believed that introduction of air power would escalate the conflict. According to a report, it was Gen. V.P. Malik who convinced Air Chief Marshal A.Y. Tipnis to include air support on May 24, 1999, after which both made an appeal to the CCS.[93]

Air strikes started only on May 26, 1999. The reasons for the delayed use of the air force are many. First, realization on the extent of infiltration came in late. Second, as discussed earlier, the Indian political leadership was apprehensive that the use of air power might send wrong signals and escalate the conflict. It was also reported that the Indian army was initially reluctant to involve the air force.[94]

The IAF used MiG-21s, MiG-27s and improvised Mi-17

---

92. "CIA's Missing Afghan Stingers Land in Kargil," *The Indian Express*, June 7, 1999.
93. Joshi and Baweja, "Blasting Peace," 15.
94. According to Praveen Swami, who has been reporting on militancy in Kashmir for more than a decade, the Indian army was "perhaps driven by a misplaced sense that Jammu and Kashmir was the Army's exclusive concern." He wrote that during the second half of 1998, when there were credible reports about the militants acquiring SAMs, S.K. Sareen, the then air force chief, "offered the use of jaguar aircraft with photo-reconnaissance kits for surveillance...Malik declined the offer." Praveen Swami, "The Bungle in Kargil," *Frontline* 16, no. 13 (July 2, 1999).

helicopter gun ships.[95] On average, forty sorties were carried out every day.[96] From May 30 onwards, the IAF started using Mirage-2000 planes. In all, 550 strike, 150 reconnaissance, and 500 escort missions, along with 2,185 helicopter sorties, were carried out.[97]

Air attacks and surveillance by Indian Air Force were limited to its side of the LoC. Though occasional straying to the other side of the LoC might have occurred, there was a deliberate attempt by Indian political and military high commands to keep the air operations contained to the Indian side of the LoC. The reasons are not difficult to decipher. First, this was pursuant with its larger strategy of keeping the conflict limited within its territory. Second, any air operation across the border would have escalated the conflict, a result for which Pakistan had been hoping. The fact that the infiltrators were armed with Stinger missiles is proof that the planners of the Kargil incursion expected the use of air power. Before India even started contemplating the use of its air power on May 22, 1999, Brig. Rashid Qureshi, Director General of Inter Service Public Relations (ISPR) made a statement that "no violation of Pakistani air space will go unnoticed."[98] He also stated, "Placing of fighter squadrons on high alert [in India] is a threat to us [Pakistan]."[99] Earlier, the Indian Air Force had placed two of

---

95. The Mi-17 helicopter, made by Russians, was originally a transport helicopter used for ferrying soldiers and supplies. The IAF improvised them by fitting rocket pads. "Mi-17 Modified for Strike Operations," *The Times of India*, May 29, 1999.
96. Harinder Baweja and Ramesh Vinayak, "Peak by Peak," *India Today* 24, no. 24 (June 14, 1999): 18.
97. "The Action Theatre," 20.
98. Shakil Shaikh, "PM, COAS Discuss Indian Build-up at LoC," *The News*, May 23, 1999.
99. Since the air power was not used against the militancy in Jammu and Kashmir by India, Pakistan perceived India's objective to keep two IAF squadrons on high alert was against Pakistan's security interests. Shaikh, "PM, COAS Discuss Indian Build-up at LoC."

its fighter squadrons on alert for "possible strike operations" in Kashmir's Dras-Kargil-Batalik region.[100] Third, the shooting down of two Indian MiG aircrafts and a helicopter by Pakistan made India extremely cautious.[101] Besides the economic costs, the psychological costs of losing an aircraft and its impact on the morale of the troops and infiltrators might have factored into the cautious use of air power against the infiltrators.

The Use of Manpower

What numbers were involved in the fighting on both sides? Indian estimates of the number of infiltrators varied. Initially India believed that not more than a few hundred had infiltrated. On May 24, one day before the crucial CCS meeting and two days before the initial use of air power, it was estimated that there were around 300 militants on the various heights based on satellite pictures.[102] By the first week of June 1999, the Indian army believed that there were 700 infiltrators.[103] During the same period, India had already mobilized 20,000 men into the conflict zone.[104] By the second week, the estimated number of militants rose to 1,000.[105]

By the last week of June, the numbers rose even further and India became convinced that the infiltrators included both

---

100. "IAF Squadrons on Alert as Kargil Face-off Continues," *The Times of India*, May 21, 1999.
101. On May 27, 1999, two MiG-21s were shot at. While the first one hit the flight carrying Sq. Leader Ojha and killed him, the second flight—according to Indian officials—developed technical problems, leading to its pilot Flt. Lt. Nachiketa ejecting, only to be captured by Pakistani forces. For accounts of these events, see "Aircrafts Were within LoC," *The Hindu*, May 29, 1999; "IAF Loses Two Aircraft in Action," *The Hindu*, May 28, 1999; "One IAF Pilot in Pak Custody," *The Hindu*, May 29, 1999; "Anza Missiles Used to Down Indian Jets," *The News*, May 28, 1999. On May 28, 1999, the infiltrators shot down a Mi-17 helicopter. See "IAF Copter Shot Down," *The Hindu*, May 29, 1999.
102. "Army Closing in on Infiltrators," *The Hindu*, May 24, 1999.
103. Baweja and Vinayak, "Peak by Peak," 18.
104. Ibid.
105. Manoj Joshi and Raj Chengappa, "The Marathon War," *India Today* 24, no. 25 (June 21, 1999): 13.

Pakistani soldiers and *mujahideen*. A news report based on the Indian army's air and field observations reported that the infiltrators could be in the range of a brigade (three battalions) or around 2,500 fighters.[106] However, in the final tally, it was estimated there were 1,500 infiltrators opposed by 20,000 Indian troops.[107]

The only authoritative account of the conflict from the Pakistani side was published later by Brig. Shaukat Qadir in 2002. According to him,

> The total number of troops [from Pakistan's side] occupying [the posts in Kargil] never exceeded 1,000 from all ranks. Four times this number provided the logistical backup to undertake the operation.[108]

Table 2.4: The Ghosts of Kargil

	Indian Casualties		Pakistani Casualties	
	Dead	Injured	Dead	Injured
6 June 1999[109]	51	230	200	
11 June 1999[110]	98	317	250	
24 June 1999[111]	175	550	350	700
12 July 1999[112]	398	578	691	
Final Figures[113]	**524**	**1365**	**737[114]**	

106. "Pakistan Intrusion in Kargil at Brigade-level," *The Indian Express*, June 26, 1999.
107. "The Action Theatre," 20.
108. Shaukat Qadir, "An Analysis of the Kargil Conflict 1999," *RUSI Journal* (April 2002): 26.
109. "'Clear Proof' of Pak. Role," *The Hindu*, June 6, 1999.
110. Data based on Joshi and Chengappa, "The Marathon War," 11.
111. Data based on Raj Chengappa, Rohit Saran, and Harinder Baweja, "Will the War Spread?" *India Today* 24, no. 27 (July5, 1999): 12.
112. According to the Indian army, the final human cost of the Kargil war was as follows: on the Indian side 398 killed, including 23 officers, 16 JCOs and 359 other ranks, while 578 were injured. See "Dateline Kargil-VIII," http://www.armyinkashmir.org/articles/dateline8.html.
113. The final figures were given in the first week of December 1999, by George

The Cost of Kargil

By the second week of June 1999, it was estimated that India was spending approximately $4 million every day on the conflict.[115] According to an assessment in the third week of June, India would have spent in the range of Rupees 5,000 to 6,000 crores, if the situation dragged for three months.[116] The final cost was estimated to be Rupees 1,110 crores, or an average of Rupees 15 crores every day.[117]

India believed, as demonstrated by the statements of its finance and external affairs minister, that it could meet the economic challenge. Jaswant Singh asserted, "For us [India] the battle will be a cut in the finger. But Pakistan will bleed itself dry, if it doesn't see reason."[118]

The Threat of Escalation

Besides the actual conflict, which witnessed the use of power by both India and Pakistan, there were subtle and explicit threats of escalating the conflict into an open war between the two countries.

Fernandes, the defense minister of India, in his reply at Parliament. See *The Hindu*, December 3, 1999. The casualty includes 519 from the Indian army and five from the air force.

114. The figures for Pakistani casualties to date have not been given by its government, for obvious reasons. According to the Indian army figures, the casualty was 737 Pakistani soldiers, including 45 officers, 68 Special Service Group (SSG) soldiers, and 13 ISI personnel. See http://www.armyinkashmir.org/articles/dateline10.html.
115. "Kashmir Conflict Costs India $4 Million a Day," *The Asian Age*, June 16, 1999.
116. The ICICI Securities and Finance Company's report on debt market was quoted to have stated that the expenditure would be between 0.3 to 0.6 percent of the country's GDP. The report, however also stated, "The Kargil conflict will definitely have its cost, but the Indian economy is robust enough to bear it even if it takes a couple of months." See "Kargil Crisis to Hit Indian Economy," *Hindustan Times*, June 22, 1999.
117. "The Action Theatre," 20.
118. Joshi and Chengappa, "The Marathon War," 15.

The first major declaration of threat came from Sartaj Aziz after India launched its air attack. By then two significant meetings at the highest levels involving military and political leadership had taken place in Pakistan. The first meeting took place at the Chakala airbase on May 22, where Gen. Pervez Musharraf informed Sharif on the "high state of operational preparedness of the Pakistan armed forces."[119] The second meeting took place on May 25, the same day the Indian CCS was convening in New Delhi.[120] On May 26, claiming that as many as ten bombs fell inside "Azad Kashmir,"[121] Aziz warned, "We will take necessary steps to defend ourselves...We are retaliating and we will retaliate."[122] On the same day Brigadier Rashid Qureshi was quoted as stating that Pakistan reserved the right to "use all available options" including the use of air power.[123] Pakistan feared that the use of air power and troop mobilization by India might lead it to undertake a hot pursuit. Therefore, Pakistan decided to keep its troops on high alert.[124] Pakistan also expected that India might capture certain posts in "Azad Kashmir" to divert attention from India's internal political problems.

On June 6, 1999, Nawaz Sharif announced, "Chances of a

---

119. Shaikh, "PM, COAS Discuss Indian Build-up at Kargil."
120. The meeting that took place at Islamabad was chaired by the prime minister and was attended by Pakistan's foreign minister, Kashmir affairs minister, defense secretary, acting army chief, DGMO, and the commander of 10 Corps. See Shakil Shaikh, "Pak Armed Forces Put on High Alert," *The News*, May 26, 1999.
121. "Pakistan Reserves Right to Retaliate: Foreign Office," *The News*, May 27, 1999.
122. "Pakistan Warns India," *The Statesman*, May 27, 1999.
123. "Pakistan Reserves Right to Retaliate."
124. Brigadier Qureshi was quoted as saying: "Yes, there is a possibility of hot pursuit, as Pakistan has done advance planning to defend every inch of its territory. We are aware of the whole situation and our land and air forces are in a state of high alert." See Shakil Shakih, "India Uses Weapons Akin to Nerve Gas Bombs," *The News*, May 27, 1999.

war between Pakistan and India cannot be ruled out." However, the very next day Sharif withdrew the statement and said that Pakistan was not in favor of developing the situation into a full-scale war.

Besides this saber rattling, were there attempts by Pakistan to escalate the conflict? Throughout the conflict, Pakistan accused India of escalating the conflict. Munir Akram, Pakistan's ambassador to the United Nations, stated, "The present crisis in Kashmir has been caused by India's over-reaction to a military reversal in its Kashmir war and by its effort to involve and attack Pakistan in an attempt to explain this reversal to its public opinion."[125] Tariq Altaf, Pakistan's Foreign Ministry spokesman, accused India of being "on the warpath." A news report warned India of Pakistan's Special Services Group (SSG) preparing to launch an airborne assault in Ladakh.[126] There was another report claiming that the Indian army had found a plan to grab Turtok in Ladakh and integrate it with its Northern Areas.[127] Pakistan also warned of "more Kargil-like" situations.[128]

India deliberately downplayed the threats of escalation.[129] Irrespective of the pressure from within, the political leadership refused to permit crossing the Line of Control, despite the fact that it was believed that unless there was a "swift surgical strike" across the LoC, the supply lines of the infiltrators could

---

125. "Indo-Pak Duel at UN over Kargil," *The Pioneer*, June 6, 1999.
126. "Pak Troops Planning Airdrop in Ladakh?" *The Indian Express*, June 10, 1999.
127. "Indian Army Foils Pak's Game Plan," *The Hindu*, June 13, 1999.
128. Though Sharif made the statement that if the Kashmir issue was not to be resolved "according to the wishes of Kashmiri people, many more Kargil like issues can crop up," some experts in India interpreted it as Pakistan's threat to escalate the conflict by opening new fronts. See "Sharif Warns of More Kargil-like Situations," *The Times of India*, June 21, 1999.
129. See "India Dismisses Chances of War with Pak," *The Hindu*, June 7, 1999.

never be stopped.[130] The pressure came from security experts, including former military high commands, and also from political leaders. Gen. Shankar Roy Chowdhury, former Indian Chief of Army Staff, said that it was "an impractical proposition for the Army to flush out the intruders without crossing the LoC." Gen. V.N. Sharma, who was the COAS before Chowdhury, asserted that "without crossing the LoC and encircling them would mean a lot of casualties, which is not a strong military tactic."[131] Popular pressure to expand the war and cross the LoC was enormous. An article that appeared in *The Pioneer* summed up the emotional popular response. It read:

> Six of our soldiers were brutally hacked by the enemy troops. They were not killed in firing. They were chained, burnt by cigarette butts; their eyes were gouged out, their ears, noses and genitals chopped while they were alive. There could only be few parallels of such barbarism between two nations who are otherwise talking of friendship . . . And it is all Pakistan's creation. Not ours. Not at all. Now tell Sartaj Aziz to go back. Tell him, we will talk to him when we throw his troops out of our home. Don't give them any safe passage. Catch them alive or dead. Rub it into Aziz. What are we going to talk anyway? The line of control is debatable? That the death of our men is merely statistics? That the areas captured by Pak brigands can be negotiable? That there is no war? Don't confuse the military. It is already very confused by the political double talk. Let them do their duty. They know how to do it. They have a task and they will complete it. They offer no excuses. But they don't want their hands tied either. Untie their hands. Let them fight the war as it should be. Our soldiers are not fodder for Pak cannons. Let them fight the enemy as an enemy. Don't show him the Line of Control. Pakistan still has supply routes, ammunition dumps stores, artillery guns, all positioned just inside their LoC. Those are the critical targets. The enemy has to be starved, confused and the only way to do is to hit the nerve center. No amount of bombing the

---

130. "Quick Strike on the Camps across LoC is the Only Answer," *The Asian Age*, June 15, 1999.
131. "India May Have to Cross LoC: Experts," *Hindustan Times*, June 21, 1999.

> heights would achieve anything if the enemy troops manage to get their supplies of ammunition and storage regularly. We must choke them. And choking cannot be done by letting them stand and take pot shots at us while our men die in dozens. We cannot let the sacrifices go un-acknowledged. For every drop of blood shed by our men, thousand drops should be extracted from across the border. The bus can wait. It is a question of a nation's self-esteem. A nation without self-esteem is not worth dying for.[132]

Others, however, felt that India should not cross the LoC, but finish the war fast and get back to the dialogue process initiated in Lahore. In its perceptive editorial, the *Hindustan Times* summed up why India should not cross the LoC while fighting the war:

> It is not the government which is fighting the LoC battle, but the entire country. Rather than encourage postures of belligerence and warmongering, the government should go in for an early swift achievement of its basic aim of regaining total control over the area on Indian side of the Line of Control. Any extension of conflict to other areas or a protracted war would not only be at an unbearable cost to the nation but also result in the erosion of international support to media. Kargil is a fight to win back territory, but the Lahore process aims at winning hearts and minds. It should not be allowed to supersede the gains and relevance of the latter.[133]

The strategic community, though divided over the means, was united over the end—that the infiltrators should be cleared off and the LoC should be respected by Pakistan.[134] There was

132. Wilson John, "Enough, Now Teach them a Lesson," *The Pioneer*, June 11, 1999.
133. Editorial, "Crossing the Line," *Hindustan Times*, June 25, 1999.
134. See Editorial, "Clear Line," *The Times of India*, June 5, 1999; V.R. Raghavan, "The Larger Purpose in Kargil," *The Hindu*, June 5, 1999; K. Subrahmaniyam, "Advice for Mr. Aziz," *The Times of India*, June 7, 1999; V.R. Raghavan, "More Than One Offensive Needed," *The Times of India*, June 8, 1999; Editorial, "Keep Pushing ahead," *The Hindu*, June 16, 1999; Siddharth Varadarajan, "Don't Escalate Kargil to All-out War," *The Times of India*, June 18, 1999; Sanjoy Hazarika, "The LoC Is a Border, and India Will Control It," *The Asian Age*, June 19, 1999; Editorial, "Swearing by LoC," *Hindustan Times*, June 22, 1999.

Table 2.5: Action and Reaction during Kargil

Date	Action	Objectives	Reaction	Perception	Escalation Control
Second week of May	Pakistani rangers resort to shelling along the LoC on Kargil sectors	To provide cover for the infiltrators	Counter shelling from India	Normal shelling along the LoC	Indian PM speaks to Pak PM over phone
Third week of May	Two fighter IAF squadrons in Srinagar placed on high alert	To be used against the infiltrators on Kargil-Dras-Batalik sectors	Pakistan perceives it as a threat	India never used air forces against the militants; hence Pakistan perceived it as a threat	
26-29 May 1999	Air strikes by India against the infiltrators	To evict the infiltrators; to cut their supply lines; and to provide cover to the advancing Indian troops	Brig. Rashid Qureshi says Pakistan reserved the right to "use all available options" Pakistan shoots	Use of air force and the subsequent escalation was "unwarranted" Falling of around ten	The DGMOs of India and Pakistan establish

Table 2.5: Action and Reaction during Kargil

Date	Action	Objectives	Reaction	Perception	Escalation Control
			down two MiG aircrafts killing Sq. Leader Ojha and capturing Flt. Lt. Nachiketa	bombs on "Azad Kashmir" was a clear "violation of the LoC"	contact on hotline Sharif decides to send Sartaj Aziz to New Delhi to deescalate the situation

pressure on the government to give the Indian military a free hand to drive the infiltrators away.[135]

Threat of Nuclear Weapons

What role did nuclear weapons play before and during the Kargil conflict? Was Kargil a result of the nuclear tests carried out by India and Pakistan in 1998? Or, were nuclear weapons just one of several factors in Pakistan launching the infiltration? Did the presence of nuclear weapons deter India and Pakistan from escalating the conflict, thereby keeping the conflict limited?

Strategists differ in their opinion on the role of nuclear weapons in Kargil. V.R. Raghavan argued:

> The defence of national interest, nevertheless, cannot justify a recourse to nuclear weapons. On the other hand, nuclear weapons did not deter Pakistan from launching the offensive. One can even conclude that nuclear weapons encouraged it to think otherwise. The limits of the "currency of power," which nuclear weapons signify in some circles, are made apparent in Kargil.[136]

India neither contemplated the use of nuclear weapons nor gave any threat of their use during the conflict. Pakistan, on the other hand, issued threats even at the highest levels. Nawaz Sharif was the first to make a veiled threat. On May 27, 1999, he stated: "Last year's [1998] nuclear tests have given Pakistan the confidence to counter 'any enemy attack'.... They [the people of Pakistan] are confident for the first time in their history that in the eventuality of an armed attack, they will be able to meet it on equal terms." But the threat was defensive and not offensive. Confidence gained from the 1998 nuclear

---

135. See Maj. Gen. Ashok Mehta, "Let Army Decide on Safe Passage," *Hindustan Times*, June 4, 1999; John, "Enough, Now Teach them a Lesson"; Editorial, "The Only Choice," *Hindustan Times*, June 14, 1999.
136. V.R. Raghavan, "Strategic Pointers from Kargil," *The Hindu*, June 28, 1999.

tests could be used by Pakistan only against any attack on it by India and not vice versa.

Pakistan's Foreign Secretary Shamsad Ahmad was the second to issue another veiled threat on the use of nuclear weapons. On May 30 he warned: "We [Pakistan] will not hesitate to use any weapon in our arsenal to defend our territorial integrity."[137]

Was it just rhetoric or a real threat? Did Pakistan ever contemplate the use of nuclear weapons during the Kargil conflict? Did India ever believe that during the conflict Pakistan would really use nuclear weapons? The military in India and Pakistan, who were either a part of the conflict or witnessed it from close quarters, do not believe that there was ever a nuclear threat during the crisis.[138] The alarm was raised first in the United States.

According to Bruce Riedel, the day before Sharif arrived in the United States for the meeting with Clinton at Blair House on July 4, "More information developed about the escalating military situation in the area—disturbing evidence that the *Pakistanis were preparing their nuclear arsenals for possible deployment.*"[139]

---

137. "Pakistan May Use Any Weapons: Shamshad," *The News*, May 31, 1999.
138. This belief was expressed in personal interviews and discussions conducted by the author with retired military personnel from India and Pakistan. It is surprising and encouraging to find the faith that each side has with respect to the other over the use of nuclear weapons. The underlining argument is that both sides perceive the other side as "crazy enough" to go for war, but not "crazier enough" to use nuclear weapons.
139. Bruce Riedel was the Special Assistant to President Bill Clinton and Senior Director for Near East and South Asia Affairs in the National Security Council when the crisis took place. He was present along with Ambassador Karl Inderfurth and Strobe Talbott when the meeting between Clinton and Sharif took place on July 4, 1999. See Bruce Riedel, "American Diplomacy and the 1999 Kargil Summit at Blair House," Policy Paper Series (Center for the Advanced Study of India, University of Pennsylvania), 8.

Many inside the Clinton administration believed that India and Pakistan were close to nuclear exchange during the Kargil conflict. According to Riedel, "The United States was alarmed from the beginning of the conflict because of its potential for escalation...*The nuclear scenario was obviously very much in our minds*."[140] In that crucial meeting of July 4, 1999, Sandy Berger, according to Riedel, opened the session by "telling the President that this could be the most important foreign policy meeting of his Presidency because the *stakes could include a nuclear war*."[141] Later a "senior" official in the Clinton administration was quoted as saying that the conflict in Kargil "could have escalated out of control...[and] *could have brought in nuclear weapons*, without either party deciding that it wanted to go to nuclear war."[142]

India's response to the nuclear threat from Pakistan was measured. It downplayed the nuclear threats, while issuing adequate counter responses. *The Times of India* noted: "Common sense suggested that the remark be discounted. A country resorting to nuclear blackmail is not likely to make its foreign secretary the mouthpiece for the threat."[143] In retrospect, Shaukat Qadir believed that during the conflict "war, let alone nuclear war, was never a possibility."[144] Except for some background reports in the United States, it appears there was no credible threat of the use of nuclear weapons during the conflict.

Besides nuclear weapons, there were suspicions about the potential use of chemical weapons. Both India and Pakistan

---

140. Riedel, "American Diplomacy and the 1999 Kargil Summit," 3-4.
141. Ibid., 8.
142. John Lancaster, "Kashmir Crisis Was Defused on the Brink of War," *Washington Post*, July 26, 1999.
143. "Crying Nuclear Wolf," *The Times of India*, June 2, 1999.
144. Qadir, "An Analysis of the Kargil Conflict," 26.

suspected that the other would use chemical weapons. After recovering gas masks from Pakistan's Northern Light Infantry soldiers fighting in Kargil, India feared that the infiltrators had planned to use chemical weapons.[145] However, Indian army spokesman Col Bikram Singh stated that they had "not found any evidence" of chemical weapons, but believed they could have had chemical weapons as the Indian army had recovered masks from the infiltrators.[146]

Pakistan also feared that the Indian army was using chemical weapons; it sent shells landing in its territory for chemical tests.[147] India is believed to have used napalm. Quoting an official, one newspaper report stated that the MiG-27s were used to drop "500 kg fuel-air explosive (napalm) bombs on suspected hideouts in Batalik sector."[148] A news report from Pakistan asserted that India was using "weapons akin to 'nerve gas bombs' against Kashmiri Mujahideen."[149]

Objectives: Limited or not?

What were the objectives of India and Pakistan before and during the Kargil conflict? And how did they each perceive the objectives of the other? What were the different political and military objectives? Were they limited?

How did India see the Kargil conflict, in terms of Pakistan's objectives? According to a news report, based on intelligence inputs, Kargil was to be a three-phased plan. It stated:

---

145. "Army Recovers Gas Masks from Pak Soldier," *The Times of India*, June 15, 1999.
146. "Pak Intruders Had Chemical Weapons: Army," *The Times of India*, July 19, 1999.
147. "Pakistan Sends Indian Shell for Chemical Tests," *The Times of India*, June 15, 1999.
148. "IAF Drops Napalm on Hideouts," *The Pioneer*, May 3, 1999.
149. Shakil Shaikh, "India Uses Weapons Akin to Nerve Gas Bombs," *The News*, May 27, 1999.

> During the first phase, which is the boldest, Islamabad is seeking separation of the Kashmir valley from Ladakh. Simultaneously, it is making a concerted effort to entrench itself along the fulcrum of Chorbatla and Turtuk, northeast of Kargil. In the second phase, it has visualized sending in troops through the Chorbatla pass, northeast of river Indus. From here its forces could begin a thrust through the "funnel" of Turtuk along the Shyok river to Khalsar where it meets the Nubra river. India's hold over Siachen would then become untenable. In the third and final stage, Pakistan would seek to consolidate itself and completely de-link Ladakh from the rest of India incrementally.[150]

The predominant belief in India on the objectives of Pakistan's infiltration was based on the above lines—that Pakistan wanted to cut the NH-1A, which passes through Kargil from Srinagar to Leh. By doing so, Pakistan would be able to cut the supply lines to Indian troops in Siachen, making the Indian hold over Siachen difficult.[151] This in turn would "achieve a better bargaining position for a possible trade-off against the positions held by India in Siachen."[152]

The second belief was that Pakistan wanted to internationalize the Kashmir issue by involving the United Nations and other major powers.[153]

The third was to "give a fillip to militancy in Jammu and

---

150. Atul Aneja, "Pakistan Had Three-phased Plan?" *The Hindu*, June 23, 1999.
151, See Raja Mohan and Atul Aneja, "Janus Faced Pakistan," *The Hindu*, June 13, 1999; Chandra B. Khanduri, "The Intrusion in Kargil," *Hindustan Times*, June 18, 1999; J.N. Dixit, "Invasion of Kargil," *Hindustan Times*, June 23, 1999. The Kargil Review Committee (KRC) also found this as a part of Pakistan's military objectives. It said the military objectives were "to interdict the Srinagar-Leh road by disrupting vital supplies to Leh; to outflank India's defenses from the South in Turtok and Chalunka sectors through unheld areas, thus rendering its defenses untenable in Turtok and Siachen." See Kargil Review Committee Report, *From Surprise to Reckoning* (New Delhi: Sage Publications, 2000).
152. Kargil Review Committee Report, *From Surprise to Reckoning* (New Delhi: Sage Publications, 2000).
153. Invariably there is unanimous belief that one of Pakistan's clear objectives

Kashmir by military action designated to weaken the counter insurgency grid by drawing away troops from the Valley to Kargil. It would also give a boost to the morale of the militants in the Valley."[154]

In retrospect, it appears that the main objectives of Pakistan in initiating the conflict were the second and third ones, while the first was meant to be a part of its strategy. During the conflict, Pakistan repeatedly asked for the involvement of the international community so as to find a solution to Kashmir.[155] The primary objective of Pakistan in Kargil was to internationalize Kashmir and a corollary of this objective was to provoke India to retaliate, so that Kashmir would become a nuclear flash point and thereby get internationalized. Three factors figured in Pakistan's attempt to internationalize Kashmir at this juncture in 1999—the internal situation in Kashmir, which was improving slowly but steadily; general international response to Kashmir; and implications of any improved Indo-Pak relations on Kashmir.[156]

---

was to internationalize Kashmir. According to the Kargil Review Committee Report, one political and strategic motive was to "internationalize Kashmir as a nuclear flashpoint requiring urgent third party intervention." See Kargil Review Committee Report, *From Surprise to Reckoning*. The independent analysts also shared the same view. See "Clear Line," (editorial), *The Times of India*, June 5, 1999.

154. Kargil Review Committee Report, *From Surprise to Reckoning*.
155. On May 26, 1999, Tariq Altaf asked for a neutral force to check the facts on infiltrators requesting the United Nations Military Observer Group in India and Pakistan (UNMOGIP) or UN Secretary-General Kofi Annan to send observers. See "Pakistan Reserves the Right to Retaliate," *The News*, May 27, 1999. Sartaj Aziz repeated the same request of the United Nations on May 27, this time to send a special representative. See "Sartaj for UN Special Representative in Kashmir," *The News*, May 28, 1999. On May 28 Sharif stated that he had sent a letter to the United Nations requesting its mediation and accusing India of rejecting any third party mediation, which is the "global trend for mediated settlement of conflicts and disputes." See "Pakistan Calls for UN Intervention," *The News*, May 29, 1999.
156. Suba Chandran, "Why Kargil: Pakistan's Objectives and Motivations," in *Kargil: The Tables Turned*, eds. Maj. Gen. Krishna and P.R. Chari (New Delhi: Manohar Publishers, 2001): 33

After elections in 1998, the situation inside Kashmir began returning to normalcy, irrespective of occasional violent incidents. Cinema halls were opened in Srinagar after nine years; tourism was picking up; industrial houses inside India were willing to invest in the Kashmir Valley; and the Pandits were thinking about returning to their homeland.[157] Local support for militancy was on the decline and most of the militants were non-Kashmiris.[158] At the international level, all major powers, including the United States, Russia, China, and France, were in favor of resolving Kashmir at a bilateral level.[159] It was clear to Pakistan that unless something dramatic was done, militancy might die a natural death in Kashmir.

The military leadership in Pakistan, according to Shaukat Qadir, based its arguments for an operation in Kargil on the same. According to Qadir, during November-December 1998, Sharif was presented with the argument that "the freedom struggle in Kashmir needed a fillip, which could be provided by an incursion into these temporarily unoccupied territories" in the Kargil area.[160]

---

157. See the following: "Turnaround in J&K," *The Pioneer*, August 11, 1998; Prem Shankar Jha, "Kashmir Then and Now," *The Hindu*, July 24, 1998; Elisa Patnaik, "Tourism Slowly Picking up," *The Asian Age*, September 13, 1998; "Kashmir Takes a Step towards Industrial Revival," *The Economic Times*, October 5, 1998; "Plan to Help Kashmir Pandits Return to the Valley," *The Statesman*, December 26, 1998.
158. See the following reports and articles: "Local Support to J&K Ultras at an All-time Low," *The Hindu*, October 6, 1998; "Foreign Mercenaries Hijack J&K Secessionism," *Hindustan Times*, September 17, 1998; "Pak Hand Visible in Kashmir Insurgency," *The Hindu*, July 15, 1998.
159. For the views of these countries see Chandran, "Why Kargil: Pakistan's Objectives and Motivations," 36-37.
160. Qadir, "An Analysis of the Kargil Conflict," 26. Qadir also says, "The military leadership had not presented a complete analysis of the scale of operation or its possible outcome, nor had they set out its political aim and how it would be achieved."

According to Qadir, the political and military objectives of Pakistan's Kargil policy were the following:

> The political aim underpinning the operation was "to seek a just and permanent solution to the Kashmir issue in accordance with the wishes of the people of Kashmir." However the military aim that preceded the political aim was "to create a military threat that could be viewed as capable of leading to a military solution, so as to force India to the negotiating table from a position of weakness."[161]

The objective of Pakistan in initiating the conflict at Kargil was neither territorial nor military; rather, it was political. Revival of militancy in Kashmir, thereby keeping the Kashmir issue alive at bilateral and international levels, was the main objective of the infiltration. Holding the Kargil heights was a tactic, and thus not the objective of the plan. Interdicting the NH-1A was another tactic and it is doubtful whether the Pakistani military really believed that they could do so without escalating the conflict.

The strategic objectives, tactics, and terrain were chosen carefully by the planners of the Kargil infiltration, in order that the entire conflict would be kept limited without escalating into an open conflict between India and Pakistan. Clearly, it was a limited conflict, if not limited war, that the planners had in mind. The strategic objectives, as seen earlier, were political and limited. They were aimed at internationalizing the Kashmir issue by giving a fillip to militancy in the Kashmir Valley. The tactics, too, were limited. Pakistan was well aware that any explicit involvement of its regular troops was tantamount to an open war, and hence chance of its escalation. If troops belonging to either its army or paramilitary were to be involved, then it would give India a free hand to cross over the LoC, as it would be considered an act of war. It would also

161. Ibid., 27.

exert enormous pressure on Pakistan at the international level. Ultimately, though none of the major countries believed that the infiltrators were *mujahideen*, during the initial period Pakistan was able to hoodwink the international community that its troops were not party to the operations. Pakistan was also able to mobilize internal support for the operations, as many Pakistanis believed that the infiltrators were in fact *mujahideen* who were fighting the Indian oppression with a renewed vigor and a new strategy. It is doubtful whether the Pakistanis would have seen the infiltration and the subsequent conflict favorably if they knew it was their troops that were fighting in Kargil. Also it was doubtful whether Sharif would have ever agreed to such an operation. If the Lahore declaration, the Mishra-Naik negotiations, and Sharif's frantic efforts towards the end of June 1999 are taken into account, one can safely conclude that he was genuine towards reaching an agreement on Kashmir with Vajpayee.

There was no plan to hold the heights permanently by the Pakistani infiltrators. Holding the heights was a tactic to highlight the Kashmir issue; hence Pakistan decided to vacate once the objective was achieved. While no one could undermine the efforts taken by the Indian military and their sacrifices, Pakistan could have increased casualties to a considerable level and prolonged the conflict, by continuing logistical support for the infiltration. Though India succeeded in recapturing a major chunk of the occupied peaks, as of July 5, the conflict was not over.

At no time did Pakistan want to expand the conflict. It was focused only on Kargil. There is no reason to believe that the planners ever thought of using nuclear weapons. The occasional threat of use of nuclear weapons, as has been discussed earlier, was a political stunt and was never real.

Table 2.6: Pakistan and the Kargil Conflict

	Nature	Notes/Remarks
Strategic Objectives	Limited	To internationalize Kashmir To revive militancy in Kashmir, which was declining by 1998
Tactics	Limited	To call for international mediation To call for UN intervention To hold a few peaks in Kargil sector To force India to retaliate To limit India's response inside Indian side of the LoC
Manpower	Limited	Involved 1,000-1,500 regular troops, with approximately 4,000 support troops, in the guise of *mujahideen* Few *mujahideen* providing logistic support
Terrain	Limited	Focused only on four sectors—Mushkoh Valley, Dras, Kaksar and Batalik
Weapons	Limited	Machine guns, artillery, Stinger and Anza missiles
Duration	Limited	The infiltration was not aimed at capturing the peaks and altering the LoC in Pakistan's favor
Civilian Control	Limited	Though Sharif was told about the operation, he was never briefed on the intensity and nature of it. It was an army adventure.

	The military gave up in the last week of June after realizing that its plan had in fact backfired and that at the international level it had been isolated.
Achievements / Limited Failures of Kashmir	Kargil was internationalized instead Militancy was revived in Jammu and Kashmir
	Led to a military coup in Pakistan

Why Kargil?

Kargil was chosen as a terrain for specific reasons. Why should the infiltration be undertaken in Kargil and not in Baramulla, Rajouri, or Poonch sectors? It is essential to understand that militancy has an element of local support in these other regions. The Kargil region has never witnessed any militancy and, in terms of ethnic composition and their attitude towards an independent Kashmir, the Muslims of Kargil are different from the Muslims in the Kashmir Valley. The majority in Kargil are Shia muslims and have never been a part of the militant or *azadi* movement that is centered in the Valley.

Kargil was chosen for infiltration for many reasons. First, the topography of Kargil was promising. According the Lt. Gen. Raghavan:

> This [Kargil] is the only sector on the Line of Control (LoC) where Pakistani posts have an advantage of higher positions. Elsewhere on the LoC, they are at a disadvantage since the dominating heights are held by the Indian military.[162]

The second important factor was Indian patrolling. The areas that were occupied by the infiltrators were considered

162. V.R. Raghavan, "A Turning Point in Kashmir," *Frontline* 16, no. 12 (June 18, 1999).

"unheld" by the Indian military establishment. Lieutenant General Kishan Pal, Commander of 15 Corps, is on record saying that the ground occupied by the infiltrators was of little strategic importance. His argument was,

> If I don't take notice of them, it will make no difference. If they come off the heights in the summer, they will be slaughtered. And if they don't leave them in the winter, they will freeze to death.[163]

Third, Pakistan chose to infiltrate Kargil in anticipation of the political and military pressure on India and its response. In other words, the political significance of the terrain was important. The planners were well aware that while creating enough political and military pressure on India, occupation of heights in Kargil would also make sure that the political and military response would be mild. More importantly, India would not escalate the level of conflict beyond a limited extent. Had the same plan been executed in the Baramulla or Poonch sectors, India's response would have been severe. In terms of topography, patrolling, and political sensitivity, an infiltration in these regions would have witnessed an escalation that could not have been controlled by the planners. Though prepared for air strikes and therefore armed with Stinger and Anza missiles, Pakistan actually never expected India to use air power. This could be gauged from Shaukat Qadir's explanation from his point of view on the use of air power by India in Kargil. According to him:

Within a few days, on May 28 two MIGs were shot down by Pakistan. The following day Pakistan shot down two helicopters. India's lack of success had nothing to do with the effort, but rather the nature of terrain, which ensured that bombing had little chance of working unless it was laser

163. Praveen Swami, "War in Kargil," *Frontline* 16, no. 12 (June 18, 1999).

guided—the only kind that could be accurate in this terrain. Since this terrain also made it impossible for the Indians to put troops on the ground, they tried using helicopters, which forced them to expose themselves.[164]

A fourth reason for the choice of Kargil was the timing. Occupation, detection, and counter-offensive provided an adequate timeframe in the Kargil area for a sustained escalation, which could then be controlled. Infiltration could have started some time during April 1999. According to Qadir, it was in March 1999 that "the leadership of the army was apprised of the operation and the Military Operations (MO) Directorate in GHQ [general headquarters] was tasked to evolve a strategic operational plan."[165] The infiltrators began occupying the heights in April 1999 and built bunkers. They were detected by a shepherd during the first week of May and confirmed by the Indian army during the second week of May. As seen earlier, it took time for India to realize the extent of infiltration and mobilize its troops accordingly. The escalation thus was gradual, and only Kargil could have given this slow escalation trajectory to the planners of infiltration. During this slow escalation, Pakistan attempted to internationalize Kashmir, as seen earlier, and also warned India that escalation of war to the other side was not acceptable.

In retrospect, this slow escalation trajectory would not have been available to Pakistan, had it planned the infiltration elsewhere. And it was essential for Pakistan to have this slow response, so that it could make political maneuvers at national, bilateral, and international levels.

---

164. Qadir, "An Analysis of the Kargil Conflict," 27.
165. Ibid.

Table 2.7: Pakistan's Expectation of Indian Response

Indian Response	Expected Nature	Expectation/Remarks
Use of Manpower	Limited	Since the Indian military is tied down in Kashmir already, India would not mobilize more troops in Kargil. The fear of revived militancy would force India to maintain its troop level inside the valley
		Threat of an all out-war would keep India from moving all of its troops
Use of Weapons	Limited	The terrain is unfavorable. India would use mainly its artillery
Use of Air Force	Minimal	The terrain is unfavorable for the use of the air force without crossing the LoC
Use of Diplomacy	Minimal	India would fail to convince the international community on the nature of infiltrators
Internal Political Support	Minimal	The Bharatiya Janata Party (BJP) would not be able muster enough strength to fight an all-out war with Pakistan
External Pressure	Minimum on Pakistan, but maximum on India	Internationalization would favor Pakistan, as the international community would force India to reach a consensus on Kashmir

Communication during Kargil

How much communication was there between India and Pakistan at the highest political and military levels during the conflict?

It is unfortunate that the political leadership at the highest level between India and Pakistan suspended their communication during the crisis period. The first major meeting took place between Sartaj Aziz and Jaswant Singh, Pakistani and Indian foreign ministers, respectively, on June 12. The meeting failed when both India and Pakistan saw the other sticking to their points.[166]

Who Fought from Pakistan's Side?

It was essential to analyze who the infiltrators were. Initially India thought that they were *mujahideen* who were provided with support by the Pakistan army. Until the last week of May 1999, it was believed that the infiltrators were Afghan *mujahideen*. Towards the end of May, India realized that the infiltrators also included Pakistani soldiers. On May 26, an official of the Indian Ministry of External Affairs stated that the operations involved both Pakistan army regulars and mercenaries.[167] In a statement made on June 1, Fernandes announced, "All those who have been pushed into our territory by the Pakistani side, *including Pakistani troops*, should go back across the LoC."[168]

Towards the end of the first week of June, Indian perceptions of the infiltrators changed. It now saw most of the intruders as Pakistani regulars.[169] In the first week of June, the

166. "Stalemate in Indo-Pak Talks," *The Hindu*, June 13, 1999.
167. "Intrusion Obviously Had Full Backing of Pak Govt.: India," *Hindustan Times*, May 27, 1999.
168. "Cease-fire Only after Infiltrators Quit: Fernandes," *The Hindu*, June 2, 1999.
169. "Most Intruders Are Pak Regulars," *The Statesman*, June 8, 1999.

Indian army started releasing evidence clearly pointing to the involvement of Pakistani soldiers. On June 5, the Indian army released documents of the deceased and identified their names and identity cards.[170] By the second week of June, the Indian army believed that three battalions of Pakistani regular troops were involved in the conflict. It found the 3rd, 4th, and 6th Battalions of the Northern Light Infantry, along with the Special Services Group, were involved.[171] Towards the end of the conflict, the Indian military stated that the infiltrators were composed of Pakistani regulars and not *mujahideen*. Gen V.P. Malik was quoted as saying that, based on evidence recovered from the bodies, the infiltrators were regulars from the Pakistan army and not *mujahideen*.[172]

Looking at the conflict in retrospect, according to an independent assessment based on the various captured documents, interrogation reports and personal interviews, the infiltrators "were created from four Northern Light Infantry battalions and two companies of the Special Services Group (SSG)."[173]

The government of Pakistan vehemently denied any

---

170. For example, the June 5 release mentioned the killed as Lance Naik Arbaz Khan and Sepoy Saith Khan belonging to 4- Northern Light Infantry (NLI) and Sepoy Mahboob Ali from 3-NLI. See "'Clear Proof' of Pak Role," *The Hindu*, June 6, 1999.
171. An Indian army spokesman was quoted as saying, "So far 3,4, and 6 Northern Light Infantry Battalions along with subunits of the Special Services Group and elements of supporting arms and services of the Pakistan army have been identified in the pockets of intrusion." See "Three Pak Battalions Active in Kargil Hills," *The Asian Age*, June 16, 1999.
172. "Kargil Wholly Pak Army's Deed: Gen Malik," *The Times of India*, July 19, 1999.
173. See Maj. Gen. Ashok Krishna, "The Kargil War," in *Kargil: The Tables Turned*, eds. Maj. Gen. Ashok Krishna and P.R. Chari, (New Delhi: Manohar Publishers, 2001): 100-101. According to Maj. Gen. Krishna, the four groups include 4 NLI (located in Gilgit), 6 NLI (Skardu), 5 NLI (Minimarg) and 3 NLI (Dansam).

presence of its troops, especially in the initial period. It continuously emphasized that the infiltrators were actually *mujahideen*. The public at large believed during the conflict that it was the *mujahideen* who occupied the Kargil heights.[174] One unknown militant outfit based in Pakistan, Tehrik-i-Jihad, even claimed responsibility for the infiltration.[175] It even asserted later that it was sending more fighters to "make our position stable."[176] Later, the Lashkar-e-Toiba also claimed that its cadres were fighting in Kargil and it was even reported in the *Washington Post* that it conducted training on high altitude warfare for its cadres.[177] An independent analyst, who worked with the Indian intelligence earlier, doubted that the infiltrators could be the followers of Osama bin Laden.[178] There were also news reports suggesting that Osama bin Laden was closely working with Pakistan's government to push his Islamic fighters into Kargil.[179] The British and German intelligence

---

174. See the following articles for the general perception about the infiltrators in Pakistan. Syed Alamdar Raza, "Balance of Power in Kashmir," *The News*, June 3, 1999; Khalid Mehmud, "The Kargil Scenario," *The News*, June 3, 1999; M.S. Qazi, "High Tempers at High Mountains," *The Frontier Post*, June 7, 1999; Gen. Mirza Aslam Beg, "Kargil Conflict and beyond," *The Frontier Post*, June 5, 1999; and Tanvir Ahmad Khan, "Managing the Kargil Crisis," *Dawn*, June 8, 1999.
175. "Pak Based Militant Outfit Men in Kargil," *The Hindu*, May 24, 1999.
176. "Mujahideens in Kargil Safe: Tehrik-e-Jihad," *The News*, May 27, 1999.
177. "Lashkar Conducted High-altitude Training for Infiltrators," *The Hindu*, June 8, 1999.
178. Even the government of India and its army did not share this perception. According to a former intelligence official, "It is likely that the ISI found a convenient way out of this dilemma by helping bin Laden and his followers escape from FATA to the Kargil area through the Northern Areas (Gilgit and Baltistan) and set up a fresh sanctuary in Indian territory, with the logistic and firepower backing of the Pakistani army." See B. Raman, "The Portents of Kargil," Security and Political Risk Analysis (SAPRA) India, http://www.subcontinent.com/sapra/military/img_1999_05 _001.html. Also see B. Raman, "Is Osama bin Laden in Kargil?" *The Indian Express*, May 26, 1999.
179. "Bin Laden Worked in Tandem with Pak to Push Infiltrators," *Hindustan Times*, June 15, 1999.

agencies were quoted as having reported bin Laden's involvement in Kargil.[180]

At a later stage, analysts in Pakistan and even the government of Pakistan started accepting, both directly and indirectly, that Pakistani regulars were involved. According to Shaukat Qadir, "the occupants (in Kargil) were essentially the soldiers of the Northern Light Infantry (NLI), there were some local *mujahideen* assisting as labour to carry logistical requirements."[181]

Table 2.8: Kargil as a Limited War: The Final Tally

	India	**Pakistan**
Areas of Engagement	Mushkoh Valley, Dras, Kaksar, and Batalik sectors, covering an area of 130 to 150 sq km, covering around 150 km of the LoC with a depth ranging from seven to fifteen kms from the LoC on Indian side	None
Number of Troops Engaged	20,000	1,000-1,500 (regular troops) 4,000 (providing logistic support)
Casualties	Dead: 524 Injured: 1,365	737 NA
Use of Weapons	Machine guns, Bofors guns	Stinger and Anza missiles; machine guns Helicopters

180. "German Intelligence Says Osama Is Involved in Kashmir Crisis," *The Asian Age*, June 16, 1999.
181. Qadir, "An Analysis of the Kargil Conflict," 26.

	MiG-21s, MiG-27s, Mirage 2000 and Mi-17 helicopters	
Duration	74 days	74 days
Objectives	To clear intrusion	To internationalize Kashmir To give a fillip to militancy in Jammu and Kashmir
Results	Limited success: 1. India succeeded in driving out the infiltrators. LoC got strengthened internationally 2. Failed to curb militancy, which got revived with an added ferocity, in Jammu and Kashmir	Limited failure along with limited success: 1. Internationalized Kashmir, but not according to its wishes; LoC got reaffirmed 2. Revived militancy in Jammu and Kashmir 3. Resulted in army taking over power in the long run

To conclude, three factors contributed to the emergence of the concept of limited war with Pakistan. First was the continuing political deadlock between both countries, which could not sustain a political dialogue for a longer period due to various internal and external factors. Pakistan could not be politically pressured to reach an understanding with India.

A second factor that contributed to the emergence of the limited war concept in India was the continuing militancy in Jammu and Kashmir and Pakistan's support towards the same. India's efforts either bilaterally or through exerting pressure on the international community to prevent Pakistan from supporting militancy did not yield any tangible results.

With political efforts not yielding the desirable results and with militancy continuing in Jammu and Kashmir, how was India going to put pressure on Pakistan especially from supporting militancy in Jammu and Kashmir and reach an acceptable compromise? How would India respond to Pakistan's proxy war without increasing the bilateral conflict into an all-out war? The concept of limited war emerged as a possible option. The advocates believe that such a military option would convey India's seriousness in combating Pakistansponsored militancy. Besides, the advocates also believe that such a limited military response would keep the war limited to Jammu and Kashmir and would not spread along the international border.

While the first two factors contributed to the emergence of the concept of limited war in India, it was the third factor—the Kargil War, which made India realize that a limited war along the LoC is possible. As has been discussed, the Kargil War in fact was a limited confrontation in every sense. Irrespective of occasional threats to enlarge the war either in terms of using bigger weapons, including nuclear weapons, and enlarging the theater of operations, the Kargil War remained limited.

If Pakistan could initiate and finalize a limited war on Indian soil, could the latter repeat the same on the former's soil? The advocates in India of limited war believe that India could wage a limited war vis-à-vis Pakistan, arguing that there exists sufficient space under the nuclear umbrella.

CHAPTER THREE
Limited War with Pakistan Is There Sufficient "Space"?

The Space for Limited War: Indian Perceptions

Kargil is considered an example of limited war by its advocates in India. Based on the outcome of Kargil, these advocates of limited war argue that India could fight such a war and eventually win it. According to George Fernandes:

> India's success [in Kargil] was due to the ability of our defence forces to fight and win such a limited war at a time, ground and means of fighting chosen by the aggressor. If India can beat a professional military force equipped with modern fire power, at the ground (with Pakistani forces on dominating heights) and time of Pakistani choice with the initiatives also in their hands, then India can beat Pakistan anytime, anywhere.[1]

The advocates in India of limited war against Pakistan base their arguments on the following:

- Under the nuclear umbrella, there exists a space to conduct a limited war with Pakistan.
- The political, economic, and human costs of the use of a nuclear weapon would prohibit both India and Pakistan from considering the use of nuclear weapons in any limited conflicts with each other.
- India is aware of the limits short of full-scale conflict to which Pakistan can be pushed in a limited war situation.
- US pressure on Pakistan, during any limited conflict

---

1. George Fernandes, "The Dynamics of Limited War," *Strategic Affairs*, http://www.stratmag.com/issueOct-15/ page07.htm.

situation, would constrain the latter from either expanding the conflict or from converting it into a large-scale conventional war.

- The fear of massive Indian retaliation, in case of a Pakistani first nuclear strike, would deter the latter from exploring the nuclear option.

Is the Space Sufficient?

How far are the above-mentioned assertions true? Indian theories of limited war are to a great extent founded on the same consensus that the limited war theorists of the United States had in the 1950s and '60s. But unfortunately, the "rough consensus" amongst the American theorists during that period was based on "logical speculation and inference, shaped more by politics and psychology than by science and evidence; and therefore the claims of competing strategic objectives and theories are free to reassert themselves in new forms that are always plausible in logic and unverifiable in practice."[2] Invariably, Indian theories of limited war are also based on the same logical speculation and inference and shaped by politics and psychology, rather than by any science and evidence.

Space under the Nuclear Umbrella

First, the proponents believe that there exists a space under nuclear deterrence to conduct a limited war with Pakistan. According to George Fernandes, nuclear weapons "can deter only the use of nuclear weapons, but not all and any war" and under the nuclear shadow, a "conventional war remained feasible though with definite limitations if escalation across

---

2. Robert E. Osgood, *Limited War Revisited* (Boulder, CO: Westview Press, 1979), 9.

the nuclear threshold was to be avoided."[3] In a conference organized by the Institute of Defence Studies and Analyses (IDSA) at New Delhi in January 2000, he stated: "Nuclear weapons did not make war obsolete. They simply impose another dimension of the way warfare could be conducted. The Kargil War was therefore handled within this perspective with obvious results."[4]

According to Jasjit Singh, another proponent of limited war theory, "Nuclear weapons have limited the aim, scope, and extent of war among states that possess such capabilities because of the tremendously destructive potential of such weapons."[5] Elsewhere he has also stressed that "the question that defence planners must ask themselves is: what implication does the nuclear factor have on conventional wars—and therefore, on the force structure that is needed for the future? The answer is fairly clear: the need is to prepare for a limited war."[6] There is a general belief among the proponents that "since the onset of nuclearization has rendered 'total war' unthinkable, 'Limited War' must of necessity be central to the military input into decision making."[7]

What role do nuclear weapons play in Indo-Pak conflicts? Have they been a source of stability in crisis situations between India and Pakistan? What role did they play in the previous crisis situations? Because the nuclear capabilities of India and Pakistan have been acknowledged since the second half of the 1980s, an analysis of the role of nuclear weapons in major crisis

3. "Fernandes Unveils 'Limited War' Doctrine," *The Hindu*, January 25, 2000.
4. Fernandes, "The Dynamics of Limited War."
5. Jasjit Singh, "Dynamics of Limited War," *Strategic Analysis* (October 2000):1206.
6. Jasjit Singh, "Budgeting for Security Needs," *Frontline* 15, no. 15 (July 31, 1998).
7. Firdaus Ahmed, "The Impetus behind Limited War," *Peace and Conflict* 6, no. 2 (2003): 5.

situations would be essential to find out whether nuclear weapons are a source of stability and provide adequate space for a limited war. Second, it is also essential to analyze the nature of Indo-Pak deterrence, as the space under the nuclear umbrella is based on the belief that the deterrence between India and Pakistan is functional.

Weapons of Stability or Instability?: Nuclear Weapons and Indo-Pak Crises

The first major Indo-Pak crisis since both countries were widely acknowledged as developing nuclear weapons was that of Brasstacks in December 1986. But even before, since the beginning of the 1980s, there were a number of threats about the development or use of nuclear weapons, or about attacking the nuclear installations of the other. Also, there has been a lot of rhetoric from the scientific and military establishment on the use and development of nuclear weapons and nuclear signaling towards the other. The beginning of the 1980s was crucial to the development of differing threat perceptions and the emphasis on nuclear weapons in facing those threats between India and Pakistan. Bilateral, regional, and international strategic environments shaped the threat perceptions. When the 1980s began, India was aware of the close relationship between China and Pakistan and how the former aided the latter in developing a nuclear weapons program. India was also aware of the changed US non-proliferation interests, with the Reagan administration replacing that of Jimmy Carter. The presence of Soviet troops in Afghanistan made Pakistan a frontline state again, bringing cold war politics to the subcontinent. The return of Indira Gandhi to power in India also meant the end of the short-lived nonproliferation policies of the Janata government.

The first major threat was created through a newspaper

report in the United States in December 1982. The report appeared in the *Washington Post* and suggested that India was planning to attack the uranium plant at Kahuta in March 1982.[8] According to the report:

> India's military leaders have prepared a contingency plan for a preemptive strike against Pakistan nuclear facilities and proposed such an attack to Prime Minister Indira Gandhi earlier this year, according to US intelligence sources. Gandhi decided against carrying out an attack, when she first heard the proposal nine months ago, but did not foreclose the option of striking if Pakistan appeared on the verge of acquiring nuclear weapons capability, the sources said.[9]

How true was the threat of Indian preemptive attack on the Kahuta plant in March 1982? Was India really planning to attack? It is essential to understand the regional security context in which this report appeared in the newspaper. The conflict in Afghanistan had reached its peak in 1982 and the United States had been pressurising India and Pakistan to reach an understanding between them so as to remove the Pakistani fears of fighting a war on two fronts. Between April 1981 and June 1982, India and Pakistan were engaged in an attempt to reach an understanding on signing a treaty or agreement.[10] The Indian government denied the *Washington Post* report, calling it "totally false and unfounded" and "absolute rubbish."[11]

---

8. Milton R. Benjamin, "India Said to Eye Raid on Pakistan's A-plants," *The Washington Post*, December 20, 1982.
9. Ibid.
10. In April 1981, Pakistan suggested "mutual guarantees of non-aggression and non-use of force, in the spirit of the Simla Agreement," which was formally presented to the Indian government during the same year. India in reply proposed a seven point aide-memoire. Based on the Indian government's reply, Pakistan revised the proposals in June 1982. See Suba Chandran, "Indo-Pak Summits: A Profile," in *India and Pakistan: Agra Summit and After*, eds. P.R. Chari and Suba Chandran (New Delhi: Institute of Peace and Conflict Studies, 2001), 1.
11. William Claiborne, "India Denies Plan to Hit Pakistani Nuclear Plants," *The Washington Post*, December 21, 1982.

George Perkovich, in his colossal study on India's nuclear bomb, quotes many former Indian military, political, and nuclear officials on the negative impact of such an attack. He quotes two officials. According to the first, "The question was what will happen next? In my estimate, Pakistan would go to war. The international community would condemn us for doing something in peacetime, which the Israelis would get away with but India would not be able to get away with. In the end, it will result in war." Another official was quoted as saying, "We have Muslims in India...If we cooperated with the Israelis in attacking Pakistan, it would be a huge political disaster and could cause severe internal problems."[12] Nevertheless, the fact that India purchased Jaguars in the 1980s, which had the capability to bomb the Kahuta plants, has been interpreted as an Indian strategy to attack it.

Though the issue of attacking Kahuta quickly died in 1982, it surfaced again in 1984, once again through media reports. *The Wall Street Journal* interviewed Indian Prime Minister Indira Gandhi and Pakistani President Mohammad Zia ul-Haq in July 1984. The first interview, with Indira Gandhi, was published on July 5. It was followed by the second, with Zia ul-Haq, published on July 10, 1984. Earlier, Senator Alan Cranston had submitted a report that Pakistan was engaged actively in a nuclear weapons program. According to the report on Indira Gandhi's interview,

> Asked whether, if there were conclusive proof of imminent nuclear capability in Pakistan, she would consider air strikes against Pakistan facilities such as those Israel launched against an Iraqi nuclear facility, she pondered a moment and said. "I don't know. We've never thought of it really.[13]

---

12. George Perkovich, *India's Nuclear Bomb: The Impact on Global Proliferation* (Berkeley: University of California Press, 1999), 240-241.
13. Karen Elliott House and Peter R. Kann, "Amid a Host of Problems, Indira

The same reporters who interviewed Indira Gandhi and asked the question on whether she would consider attacking Pakistan's nuclear assets interviewed Zia. They had posed the same question to Zia, as could be judged from his answer: "It is a possibility. Pakistan stands the risk of its very innocent, modest facility being subjected to an air attack by India...It is a possibility we are hoping will not materialize."[14] The third media report on the subject appeared in the *New York Times* on September 15, 1984. Commenting on a CIA brief to the Senate on Pakistan's uranium enrichment, the news report stated:

> The CIA told the Senate committee, according to two members, that it had learned from a sensistive intelligence source, that Mrs. Gandhi received recommendations this year [1984] from some senior aides that India attack the Kahuta plant to make sure that the enrichment process was not used for the development of weapons.[15]

One main reason for the renewal of this debate was what Abdul Qadeer Khan had told *Nawa-i-Waqt,* in an interview in February 1984 regarding Pakistan's enrichment capacity. Speaking cryptically, Khan said, "Pakistan has broken the monopoly on the enrichment of uranium...If in the interest of the country's solidarity the President of Pakistan were in extreme need and gave the team of scientists an important mission, it would not disappoint the nation."[16]

Did this statement create enormous threat perceptions in India? Was there an effort from the Indian side to attack the nuclear enrichment plants after Khan's interview? How did the policy makers view the statement by Khan on Pakistan's

---

Gandhi Remains Serene about the State of India," *The Wall Street Journal,* July 5, 1984.

14. Karen Elliott House and Peter R. Kann, "Zia Says Pakistan Has No Plans for Nuclear Bomb," *The Wall Street Journal,* July 10, 1984.
15. Philip Taubman, "Worsening India-Pakistan Ties Worry US," *The New York Times,* September 15, 1984.
16. "Pakistani Cites Nuclear Advance," *The New York Times,* February 10, 1984.

nuclear enrichment status? R. Venkataraman, the defense minister of India, was quoted responding to the questions in Parliament on the statements made by Dr. Khan:

> You need not match the tank with the tank and this and that...All that I am bound to do is to take note of such a situation and then make arrangements for meeting a contingency of that kind...I want to make it clear that it is the definite, determined and express policy of the Government to use nuclear energy for peaceful purposes.[17]

It is clear from the above that there were no attempts to attack the nuclear plants of Pakistan by the political establishment in India. The Indian military planners may have brought to the attention of the political leadership the various alternatives that India might pursue, in addition to specific policy options that India could adopt in case Pakistan drew closer to manufacturing nuclear weapons. These were options for emergency situations and by no means deliberate policies of the Indian government. Indira Gandhi simply rejected these options, not because she was a peacemonger, but due to the implications of such a policy. Thus, these episodes lead to a conclusion that the options may have been presented to the political leadership of India, but there were never serious efforts to pursue them. The threat of attack on the Pakistani nuclear installation by India was based on hype created and sustained by the media.

While the nuclear advocates in India and Pakistan downplayed these events in later studies, the nuclear opponents dramatized them. These incidents surprisingly were considered as part of those "six wars that never happened."[18]

---

17. Quoted in Perkovich, *India's Nuclear Bomb*, 253-54.
18. The "six wars that never happened" are discussed in the study undertaken by the leading scholars of South Asia on the Brasstacks crisis, including Kanti Bajpai, P.R. Chari, Pervaiz Iqbal Cheema, Sumit Ganguly, and Stephen Cohen. See Kanti Bajpai et al., *Brasstacks and Beyond: Perception and Management of Crisis in South Asia* (New Delhi: Manohar, 1995), 9-12.

The next major nuclear crisis in South Asia supposedly took place in 1990. In his famous article published in 1993, Seymour Hersh details the crisis as follows:

> Sometime in the early spring of 1990, intelligence that was described as a hundred percent reliable—perhaps as NSA intercept—reached Washington with the ominous news that General Beg had authorized the technicians at Kahuta to put together nuclear weapons. Such intelligence, of "smoking gun" significance, was too precise to be ignored or shunted aside. The new intelligence also indicated that General Beg was prepared to use the bomb against India if necessary. Precisely what was obtained could not be learned, but one American summarized the information as being, in essence, a warning to India that if "you move up here"—that is, begin a ground invasion into Pakistan— "we are going to take out Delhi."[19]

How accurate were Hersh's contentions? A later study carried out by scholars from India, Pakistan, and the United States asserted:

> Our assessment, after conversations with a large number of American, Pakistani and Indian civilian officials, diplomats, military and intelligence officers is that Hersh's account is largely inaccurate. It reflects the most alarmist spectrum of American views during the crisis.[20]

In his work, Raj Chengappa details how the nuclear establishment in India perceived the crisis. According to him:

> India did take the threat of a nuclear strike seriously. The armed forces, who were not briefed either about India or Pakistan's nuclear capability, were worried. V.P. Singh called S.K. Mehra, chief of air staff, and asked him whether the air force could intercept a Pakistani

---

19. Seymour Hersh, "On the Nuclear Edge," *New Yorker*, March 29, 1993, 33.
20. P.R. Chari, Pervaiz Iqbal Cheema, and Stephen Philip Cohen, *Perception, Politics and Security in South Asia: The Compound Crisis of 1990* (New York: RoutledgeCurzon, 2003), 127.

> aircraft that may be sent to launch a nuclear strike. Mehra reportedly told him that if Pakistani jets made a "bolt from the blue" strike by flying at treetop level there was no way India could prevent it. Mehra recalls: "We really didn't know if Pakistan's F-16s were capable of delivering such weapons or not. Nor were we absolutely sure of what we had. The feeling was that we were sitting ducks. It was a worrying situation for us to be in."[21]

According to Chengappa, Prime Minister V.P. Singh feared that "Pakistan would blast a nuclear weapon over their own territory and then threaten us by saying the next one would fall on us. So we decided to tell Pakistan that if they tried anything funny the damage would be devastating."[22] Singh was so serious that he asked scientific advisor V.S. Arunachalam "to keep everything ready for a nuclear counter attack."[23]

Another detailed study on the issue comments:

> It is also possible that Pakistani suggestions of nuclear delivery preparations were a colossal bluff. Without corroboration from Pakistani leaders, only a circumstantial case can be made for the claim that Islamabad devised a clever hoax to achieve its objectives in 1990. That evidence is compelling nonetheless. Pakistan certainly had a motive: it interpreted Indian deployments in Rajasthan as possible preparation for a massive conventional assault that could have severed the strife ridden Singh province from northern Pakistan. As tensions arose, Pakistani officials may have believed it necessary to do something dramatic to signal their deterrent resolve. Faking nuclear delivery preparations would have spurred the United States into action; Washington would intervene to ease the

---

21. Raj Chengappa, *Weapons of Peace: The Secret Story of India's Quest to be a Nuclear Power* (New Delhi: Harper Collins Publishers, 2000), 357.
22. Ibid.
23. However, Arunachalam did not believe that Pakistan would use nuclear weapons. He apparently told V.P. Singh: "My assessment...was that Pakistan would not use nuclear weapons." Ibid.

tension, or at least pass along its observations, who would be deterred from any aggression they might be contemplating.[24]

The last crisis in which threats of the use of nuclear weapons was involved was that of the Kargil conflict, which has been discussed in an earlier chapter of this work.

Nuclear Deterrence: Is It Functional?

How do the analysts see nuclear deterrence between India and Pakistan? In particular, how do the analysts in India and Pakistan see Indo-Pak nuclear deterrence?

To a large extent, analysts outside India and Pakistan have been influenced predominantly by how the West perceived nuclear proliferation outside the Nuclear Non-Proliferation Treaty (NPT) fold in the 1970s. Scholars outside India and Pakistan who wrote on nuclear issues could be divided into three: the n-advocates, who viewed nuclear weapons as a source of stability; the n-opponents, who perceived nuclear weapons as a source of instability; and n-apartheidists, who perceived nuclear weapons a source of stability between the United States and the Soviet Union, but as a source of instability outside, especially in the Third World.

The nuclear advocates base their argument on the fact that nuclear weapons act as a source of stability between the superpowers. Amongst these n-advocates, a sub-section has even argued that nuclear weapons may have the same effects and results elsewhere.[25] It is even believed that nuclear weapons

24. Devin T. Hagerty, *The Consequences of Nuclear Proliferation: Lessons from South Asia* (London: BCSIA Studies in International Security, 1998), 160-161.
25. Kenneth Waltz has been a leading proponent of this argument. According to him, "Nuclear weapons have reduced the chances of war between the United States and the Soviet Union and between the Soviet Union and China. One may expect them to have similar results elsewhere." See the following

would provide stability to certain regions, which are facing chronic instability.[26]

Nuclear apartheidists hold that "many of the political, technical and situational roots of stable nuclear deterrence between the United States and the Soviet Union may be absent in South Asia, the Middle East or other regions to which nuclear weapons are spreading."[27] The argument continues by asserting that due to "heightened stakes and lessened room for maneuver in conflict-prone regions, the volatile leadership and political instability...and technical deficiencies," there is "a high risk of nuclear weapons being used" outside the US-Soviet nuclear belt.[28] Devin Hagerty has summed up this view, analyzing a number of existing views and theories: "Contrary to the apparently pacifying effect of US and Soviet nuclear weapons, however, their wider spread is generally considered to be dangerous."[29]

Clearly nuclear apartheidists and nuclear opponents base their argument on two aspects: The political environment amongst rival countries in the Third World is unstable and

---

works by Waltz: *The Spread of Nuclear Weapons: More May Be Better*, Adelphi Paper 171 (London: IISS, 1981); Scott D. Sagan and Kenneth N. Waltz, *The Spread of Nuclear Weapons: A Debate* (New York: W.W. Norton & Company, 1995); "Towards Nuclear Peace," in *Strategies for Managing Nuclear Proliferation: Economic and Political Issues*, eds. Dagobert L. Brito, Michael D. Intriligator, and Adele E. Wick (Lexington, KY: Lexington Books, 1982); "What Will the Spread of Nuclear Weapons Do to the World," in *International Political Effects of the Spread of Nuclear Weapons*, ed. John Kerry King (Washington, DC: US Government Printing Office, 1979).

26. See the following works, which argue for the case of regional nuclear deterrent: William B. Bader, *The United States and the Spread of Nuclear Weapons* (New York: Pegasus, 1968); Walter B. Wentz, *Nuclear Proliferation* (Washington, DC: Public Affairs Press, 1968).
27. Lewis A. Dunn, *Containing Nuclear Proliferation*, Adelphi Paper 263 (London: IISS, 1991), 4.
28. Ibid.
29. Hagerty, *The Consequences of Nuclear Proliferation*, 11.

also lacks adequate technical development to maintain the stability and survivability of command and control structures. Of late, there has also been an emphasis on nuclear assets falling into the hands of terrorists.

It is a debatable hypothesis whether nuclear weapons in the hands of other countries are dangerous due to political stakes involved and the chronic instability amongst them. The history of cold war conflict would provide adequate examples of the high political stakes between the superpowers in Europe, Asia, and Africa. Hagerty's argument is valid and appropriate on the relations between political stakes and nuclear stability. He writes:

> It is easy for contemporary analysts to forget the profound animosities between the United States and the Soviet Union during the various crises over Berlin and Cuba or between the Soviet Union and China during the 1960s. The political stakes in the Korean peninsula, South Asia and the Middle East today do not exceed those that faced the United States, the Soviet Union and China at the height of the cold war.[30]

Besides the technical and political component of deterrence, though not explicitly stated, there is an element of downplaying the human component of nuclear deterrence in the Third World. Western analysts are also influenced by cultural factors to conclude that the political and military leadership in the developing world is more prone to use nuclear weapons. While there is much focus on the development of crisis situations, not much has been written about why and how those crises were defused. In the case of India and Pakistan, because of the fact that both countries fought each other openly thrice in the past and once not so openly; had three close encounters in the 1980s and '90s; and one country is involved

30. Ibid., 21.

in aiding a militant movement in the other, there has been a focus on the political instability argument. But why was it that none of the three open wars were blown into a full-fledged war, destroying each other completely?[31] Why did the three close encounters not develop into an open war? And what prevented the not so open conflict in 1999 and a full-scale mobilization in 2002 from developing into open war?

Efforts to reach a political understanding, whatever their outcome, have also been downplayed, so as to focus on the "unstable political environment not conducive for the presence of nuclear weapons" argument. The argument that nuclear weapons are a source of stability between the superpowers, but source of instability in the third world countries is dangerous and bogus. If political rivals in the developing world, such as India and Pakistan, reach an understanding, then would the apartheidists support the spread of nuclear weapons in these states?

How do India and Pakistan see each other on nuclear weapons? Though there seems to be overwhelming support for the possession of nuclear weapons at the popular level, the support for the same is divided at the strategic level in both countries.

Nuclear deterrence "requires the construction and maintenance of a retaliatory or second strike capability."[32] One should have a "fully deployed nuclear force...to survive a first

---

31. The wars of 1948, 1965, and 1971 ended when one party called for a cease-fire, irrespective of having advantages in the battlefield. There were no attempts to destroy the other completely in political and economic terms. An analysis of the 1971 war and the 1972 Simla agreement between the two countries would prove, irrespective of India winning the war and liberating Bangladesh, that the Simla negotiations did not aim at squeezing Pakistan. Both in 1965 and 1971, India in fact returned some of its occupied territories in Pakistan-occupied Kashmir (PoK).
32. Kanti Bajpai, "The Fallacy of Indian Deterrent," in *India's Nuclear Deterrent:*

strike designed to prevent that force from striking back."[33] Deterrence is dependent on two factors: the strategic reach and the survivability of a retaliatory force.[34] Whereas India and Pakistan both have the first, the nuclear opponents consider that the second is doubtful. They are uncertain of how dispersed the nuclear weapons of both countries are and, even if they are dispersed, it is doubtful that they would be beyond the reach of a first strike. Is this argument true? Do India and Pakistan have first strike capabilities? What role does "first strike" play in nuclear deterrence and second, what role does it play in the nuclear doctrines of India and Pakistan?

Devin T. Hagerty argues that "first strike uncertainty will deter preemptive strikes" and for the "maintenance of first strike uncertainty, only a very rough equivalence is needed to ensure that one side cannot simply overwhelm the other in a massive attack."[35]

Hagerty based his arguments on the 1962 Cuban missile crisis in which President John F. Kennedy went ahead with the naval quarantine irrespective of a US air force report on survivability of Soviet nuclear missiles.[36] He argues, "This [Cuban] episode demonstrates the implausibility of an Indian

---

Pokhran II and Beyond, ed. Amitabh Mattoo (New Delhi: Har Anand Publications, 1999), 160.

33. Gregory S. Jones, "From Testing to Deploying Nuclear Forces: The Hard Choices Facing India and Pakistan," RAND Issue Paper IP-192 (2000).
34. Bajpai, "The Fallacy of Indian Deterrent," 160. Also see Mario E. Carranza, "An Impossible Game: Stable Nuclear Deterrence after the Indian and Pakistani Tests," *Nonproliferation Review* (spring-summer 1999).
35. Hagerty, *The Consequences of Nuclear Proliferation*, 49.
36. The US air force could not promise President Kennedy that they would be able to destroy more than 90 percent of the Soviet missiles; nor could they promise that no Soviet missile "would be fired in reply by a local commander." McGeorge Bundy, *Danger and Survival: Choices About the Bomb in the First Fifty Years* (New York: Random House, 1988) quoted in Hagerty, *The Consequences of Nuclear Proliferation*, 49.

or Pakistani military planner convincing the political leadership that a preemptive nuclear strike would definitely succeed in destroying all of the other side's nuclear war heads in a first strike."[37]

How efficient are the command and control structures of nuclear forces in India and Pakistan? While some believe that the system is slowly evolving, others believe that it is not fully operational.[38]

Finally, why should Pakistan limit a war, when it is not going in its favor? Pakistan is well aware that "in a showdown involving conventional warfare, Pakistan would probably be at a disadvantage. Its military has received no new weapons from the United States in a decade. Indigenously manufactured weapons and arms supplied by China might not be sufficient to effectively ward off an attack by India, which has been buying modern weapons on the international market from a variety of sources."[39]

Is there a possibility of a limited war between India and Pakistan escalating into a nuclear war, given the present level of mutual mistrust and unstable deterrence? According to Lt. Gen. V.R. Raghavan, "A limited war on the lines of the 1971 conflict will run serious risk of escalating to a nuclear standoff, if not a nuclear exchange."[40]

Whether a limited war would escalate into a larger war

---

37. Hagerty, *The Consequences of Nuclear Proliferation*, 49.
38. See Clayton P. Bowen and Daniel Wolven, "Command and Control Challenges in South Asia," *The Nonproliferation Review* (spring-summer 1999): 25-35; and Kanti Bajpai, "The Fallacy of Indian Deterrent."
39. Husain Haqani, "War Clouds and Pakistan's Shadow," *The Indian Express*, January 3, 2003.
40. V.R. Raghavan, "Military Persuasion or Provocation," *The Hindu*, February 12, 2003.

or a nuclear war depends on the level of strategic stability, strategic parity, and strategic communication between India and Pakistan. As seen in the first chapter, these three factors played a crucial role in the limited war discourse between the then superpowers of the United States and Soviet Union. Rather than the presence of nuclear weapons alone, these three factors (which of course do have to take nuclear weapons into account) primarily provided the base for the limited war strategies. In the Indo-Pak context, these three factors are still elusive.

Economic Costs to Pakistan

Proponents of nuclear deterrence also believe that Pakistan cannot risk a total war with India, as the economic and political cost would be disastrous. When the limited war theory made its introduction in the Indian strategic calculus in 2000, the economy of Pakistan was in bad shape. However, post-September 11 events and Pakistan's willingness to join the "war against terrorism," coupled with better management of its economy, has made Pakistan stronger economically.

Pakistan's economy today is much better than it was in 1999-2000. It would be totally wrong to presume that Pakistan would not risk enlarging a limited conflict due to economic costs, since this presumption is based on conditions that have since changed significantly.

India Is Aware of the Red Line

There is a strong conviction that India is well aware of the "red line," or the limits to which conflict can be fought short of full-scale war, and it would not engage in pushing Pakistan in ways that could force the latter to use its nuclear weapons. According to K. Subrahmanyam, "The Indian armed forces are sensitive to tolerance limits of Pakistan and are not likely to force it into a situation when it would have to consider the use of nuclear weapons."[41]

There is a strong belief in India that it knows the other side; this is likewise true with Pakistan. There has been a lot of emphasis on the cultural, historical, and territorial factors that demonstrate how similar the countries are to each other. Since India and Pakistan have much in common and have been dealing with each other for a long time, there is a tendency to simplify the human equations. But the real question that needs to be looked into is, how far are these beliefs true? In other words, do Indians and Pakistanis really understand each other? To narrow the question, does the Indian political and military elite know the political and military elite of Pakistan and vice versa? In turn, does the military in each country understand each other and are they aware of what decision each would take in a crisis situation? Is there sufficient strategic communication between the two, especially during a crisis period?

There was a strong belief in Pakistan, especially among its military leadership, about how far it could push India before initiating conflicts in 1965, 1971, and 1999. Ayub Khan underestimated Lal Bahadur Shastri before initiating military operations in Kashmir in 1965; and Pervez Musharraf underestimated Vajpayee in 1999 before sending Pakistani troops to Kargil.

Explaining the mindset inside the Pakistan army before initiating the conflict in Kargil, retired Brigadier Shaukat Qadir wrote:

> Given the total ratio of forces for India and Pakistan, which was

---

41. K. Subrahmanyam, "Indo-Pak Nuclear Conflict Unlikely," *The Times of India*, January 2, 2002.

> about 2.25:1, the MO [Military Operations Directorate] concluded that the initial Indian reactions would be to rush more troops to IHK [Indian Held Kashmir], further eroding their offensive capabilities against Pakistan. As a consequence, they concluded that would not undertake an all-out offensive against Pakistan, since by doing so it would run the risk of ending in a stalemate, which would be viewed as a victory for Pakistan.[42]

Based on his discussions with senior military officials, Qadir concluded that the political objective of Pakistan when it initiated the conflict was to "seek a just and permanent solution to the Kashmir issue in accordance with the wishes of the people of Kashmir" and the military objective was to "create a military threat that could be viewed as capable of leading to a military solution, so as to force India to the negotiating table from a position of weakness."[43]

Pakistan's strategy for this limited offensive, therefore, was:

> By July (1999), the Mujahideen would step up their activities in the rear areas, threatening the Indian lines of communication at pre-designated targets, which would help isolate pockets, forcing the Indian troops to react to them. This would create an opportunity for the forces at Kargil to push forward and pose an additional threat. India would, as a consequence, be forced to the negotiating table.[44]

The plan, which Qadir considered even retrospectively as "theoretically faultless and tactically brilliant," did not pursue the path that the planners of Pakistan's military wanted it to. To their dismay, India's response was more than they

---

42. Shaukat Qadir, "An Analysis of the Kargil Conflict 1999," *RUSI Journal* (April 2002), 26. Unfortunately, there has not been much published research on Pakistan's perspective of the Kargil conflict. The only research article seems to be that of Qadir.
43. Qadir, "An Analysis of the Kargil Conflict," 27.
44. Ibid.

had expected. Irrespective of India's response, even by the end of June 1999, in his last briefing to the soon to be deposed Nawaz Sharif, General Musharraf was believed to have told the prime minister, "[Pakistan's] military did not believe that India would succeed in ousting Pakistani troops from the posts they were holding."[45]

Clearly, Pakistan has underestimated India's response in the past conflicts. Has India estimated Pakistan correctly in the past? How long would India be in a position to pursue this restraint? If there are any serious terrorist attacks on India in the future, especially on symbols of significance and national pride such as Legislative Assembly buildings and Parliament buildings, how would India react? If there were any victims as a result of such terrorist attacks on persons of high political significance, would the Indian government still stick to its restraint policy? With most of the important decisions (including the decision to go nuclear) being influenced, to a certain extent, by internal factors, there is every possibility of India undertaking a hot pursuit or surgical strikes, which would result in considerably escalating the tensions between India and Pakistan to the nuclear level.

Hence the restraint shown during the Kargil War and in the aftermath of the December 13 attack should not be taken for granted in a limited war situation. It should be emphasized that during the entire Kargil War, Pakistan did not attempt to escalate the war beyond a certain limit for various factors. Had Pakistan escalated the conflict, say with the introduction of more regular forces or with its air force, then the result could have been very different.

---

45. Qadir, "An Analysis of the Kargil Conflict," 29.

The US Pressure on Pakistan

There is a belief amongst a section in India's strategic community that the United States would never allow Pakistan to expand a war or to use its nuclear weapons. According to them, "The presence of the US fleet in the Arabian Sea is the guarantor that nuclear weapons would not be used by Pakistan."[46] Why would the United States never allow Pakistan to use nuclear weapons? The argument is, "If and when Pakistan takes out its weapons and starts readying them for firing, the US can never be sure that some of them may not be aimed at the US carriers, considering the enormous resentment among the Pakistani servicemen against the US...the US, which is keeping Pakistan under close surveillance, will destroy the Pakistani nuclear weapons through accurate non-nuclear strikes. The Pakistanis know it, the Americans know it and the Indians also know it. Therefore, there is no risk of an Indo-Pakistani conflict with the US forces present in the Arabian Sea. It is a very different scenario from all four previous wars."[47]

How much leverage does the United States have over Pakistan? While in India the general belief is that the United States has sufficient force to pressure and deter Pakistan, events in the recent past have proved otherwise. Starting with the Indian nuclear tests in May 1998, it appears that the US pressure on Pakistan, especially over Pakistan's military leadership, is limited. While the United States may have influence over the political elites of Pakistan with regard to general issues, US influence over crucial issues that Pakistan (irrespective of whether it is democratic or military) consider as vital for its survival is minimal. For example, given Pakistan's nuclear

46. Subrahmanyam, "Indo-Pak Nuclear Conflict Unlikely."
47. Ibid.

policy, the military's hold over national security policy, and its Kashmir policy—it is highly unlikely that any external force could exert sufficient pressure to alter any of these three components.

Immediately after India's nuclear tests in 1998, Clinton tried his best to prevent Sharif from following suit. According to Bruce Riedel, who was the Special Assistant to Bill Clinton and also the Senior Director for Near East and South Asia Affairs from 1997 to 2001:

> Clinton had spent days trying to argue Sharif out of testing in response and had offered him everything from a State dinner to billions in new US assistance. Deputy Secretary of State Strobe Talbott, Central Command Chief General Tony Zinni, Assistant Secretary for South Asia Rick Inderfurth and I had traveled to Islamabad to try to persuade him, but to no avail.[48]

Before the coup that deposed Sharif in 1999, the United States hinted and warned a number of times that such a course by Pakistan's military was not acceptable to it. On September 20, 1999, an official was quoted as saying that the United States would "strongly oppose" any attempt by "political and military actors" in Pakistan to overthrow the Sharif government. The official continued, "We hope there will be no return to the days of interrupted democracy in Pakistan...We would strongly oppose any attempt to change the government through extra-constitutional means."[49] The military did not listen to the warning, as subsequent events proved. Though the statement was not liked inside Pakistan[50] there was a general belief that

48. Bruce Riedel, "American Diplomacy and the 1999 Kargil Summit at Blair House," Policy Paper Series (Center for the Advanced Study of India, University of Pennsylvania), 4.
49. Shaheeh Sehbai, "US to Oppose Interruption in Democratic Process," *Dawn*, September 21, 1999.
50. Even the moderate *Dawn* newspaper questioned: "Who is the State

the United States would come to the rescue of Sharif, in case of any threat to his rule.[51] It is believed that the United States also advised Sharif against removing Pervez Musharraf, when Shabaz Sharif visited the United States during the third week of September. During the visit, Shabaz Sharif met with Strobe Talbott, Bruce Riedel, and Karl Inderfurth.[52]

Under pressure from India, the United States attempted to convince Pakistan to refrain from supporting the militants in Jammu and Kashmir. Nancy Powell, the US Ambassador to Pakistan, went on record saying that Pakistan should prevent the militants from using its territory to cross over to the LoC and fight the Indian troops in Kashmir.[53] There have been attempts from the United States since the days of Benazir Bhutto to pressure Pakistan from supporting the militancy in Jammu and Kashmir.

US influence on Pakistan is limited and at times even non-existent. Especially in terms of Pakistan's Kashmir policy and its nuclear weapons, no external force, including the United States, is able to pressure Pakistan against what it perceive as its interests. Sharif's visit to the United States in the first week of July during the Kargil conflict should not be considered as US influence or pressure to bring the conflict to an end. There

---

Department or the US government to tell Pakistan what to do? In days gone by such advice would have been considered gross interference in our internal affairs. The US obviously thinks not." "A Lecture from Washington," (editorial), *Dawn*, September 22, 1999. Also see "The Enigma of US Intercession," *The News*, September 24, 1999.

51. Imtiaz Alam, "When Words Matter," *The News*, September 24, 1999.
52. Amir Mateen, "Shahbaz Winds up US Visit," *The News*, May 17, 1999.
53. "US Envoy Tells Pakistan to Stop Infiltration," *The News*, January 24, 2003. Also, for US efforts, see "Infiltration Must End to Avoid War: Powell Sees a Way out of Crisis," *Dawn*, June 1, 2002; "Powell Expects Musharraf to Act More against Terrorists," *Hindustan Times*, January 5, 2002; "US Expects Pak to Take More Actions against Terrorists," *The Hindu*, January 6, 2002.

Table 3.1: US Pressure on Pakistan

Date/Desired Outcome	Means of Pressure	Impact/Result
May 1999 Preventing Pakistan from going nuclear	Clinton spoke to Sharif; sent Inderfurth, Riedel, and Talbott to pressure Sharif into refraining from testing	Negative Sharif went ahead with nuclear tests and conducted five tests in Chagai
Sep-Oct 1999 Preventing Pakistan army from taking over	Issued a general warning against the take over; also informed Sharif not to make the situation unstable by removing the COAS	Negative Musharraf took over power
Post Sep 11, 2001 Pursuing Osama bin Laden and the Taliban in Afghanistan	To allow the United States to use Pakistan as a base; to force Pakistan to give up its support for Taliban and to share intelligence about Osama	Positive The military regime provided all the required support
Ongoing Curbing militancy in Kashmir	Preventing Pakistan from supporting the militants	Negative

was more pressure from Sharif on Clinton to bring the conflict to an end than there was US pressure on Pakistan.

On July 4, 1999, Sharif agreed to a pull-back, as he became more worried about the situation getting out of his hand and leading to a military takeover. In retrospect, it is evident that Sharif and Musharraf had two different views before and during Kargil conflict. According to Riedel, Sharif brought his wife and children to Washington on June 4, 1999, which was a "possible indication that he was afraid he might not be able to go home if the summit failed, or that the military was telling him to leave."[54]

The Threat of Massive Retaliation

There is also a belief that Pakistan will not use its nuclear weapons because it cannot afford a second strike. According to George Fernandes, "I can't believe they would ever use [nuclear weapons] for the simple reason that they would be inviting a second strike...[which] could be devastating given Pakistan's size."[55] Former Chief of Air Staff S.K. Sareen told an interviewer that "nuclear weapons are essentially weapons of deterrence, i.e. to dissuade the enemy from using nuclear bombs. No nation can contemplate using them against another

---

54. Sharif was more concerned than the United States about reaching an agreement on July 4, 1999. It was Sharif who called for help from the United States, as "he became increasingly desperate." He called Clinton on June 2 and appealed for US intervention, on which "the President was very clear—he could help only if Pakistan withdrew to the LoC." On June 3, 1999 Sharif "was more desperate and told the [US] President he was ready to come immediately to Washington to seek [US] help. The President repeated his caution—come only if you are ready to withdraw, I can't help you if you are not ready to pull back...Sharif said he was coming and would be there on the 4th." Riedel, "American Diplomacy and the 1999 Kargil Summit," 6-8.
55. "Military Action, if Diplomatic Efforts Fail: Fernandes," *The Asian Age*, January 3, 2002.

nuclear weapon state, as the retaliation it would invite would be unbearable. For Pakistan to use nuclear weapons against India would be suicidal. Pakistan is aware of our superior nuclear capabilities, and any use by Pakistan of nuclear weapons would be self-defeating."[56]

Limitations of Indian Limited War: The Threat of Inadvertent or Deliberate Escalation

The following factors need to be taken into consideration from an Indian perspective in initiating a limited war with Pakistan.

- Internal support and pressure on the Indian political establishment, especially if the limited war is not yielding the desired results during the initial period
- External pressure on India
- Pakistan's decision to expand the war
- Popular support in Pakistan to expand the conflict
- The threat of use of nuclear weapons by Pakistan and the national and international responses
- A militant attack in the heartland of India, either on an institution or individuals

First, how much internal support would be there for India in case it decides to wage a limited war with Pakistan? India would need a powerful reason to garner enough support to initiate a limited war with Pakistan. In the last few years, there were only a few occasions in which a political sector inside India argued for a severe military response to Pakistan. All these occasions were marked by a terrorist attack either inside Kashmir or elsewhere in India.

---

56. "We Must Not Climb Down," *The Indian Express*, January 6, 2002.

Table 3.2: Possibilities of Escalating an Indo-Pak Limited War

Assumption	Possibility	Remarks/Questions
Nuclear umbrella provides space for limited war with Pakistan	Perhaps	Depends on Indian definition of limited war and the area of operations and its duration
Political, economic and human costs of enlargement would limit the war	Unlikely	Political costs of losing a limited war may force the government and military in Pakistan to expand Even the Indian government may be forced to expand, if the limited war does not go in its favor
Indian awareness of the Pakistani redline would make the former not push too far	Perhaps	What if the Pakistani military decides to escalate like that of India in 1965 and 1971? What about the Indian redline?

Assumption	Possibility	Remarks/Questions
US pressure on Pakistan will prevent the latter from expanding the Conflict	Unlikely	The US pressure on Pakistan vis-à-vis India is inadequate, if not non-existent (e.g., Pakistan's nuclear tests, Pak support for militancy in Kashmir)
The fear of massive Indian retaliation will prevent Pakistan from exploring the nuclear option	Perhaps	Depends on Pakistan's conviction regarding India's massive retaliation capacity Are the Indians convinced of their massive retaliation capacity?

The level of internal support crucial in any limited war scenario depends on other factors. First, it would depend on the level of parliamentary support that the government enjoys. Even if the government enjoys majority support in the Parliament, support from opposition parties would be vital in any war scenario. In general, the opposition parties have always been supportive of the governments during any external aggressions. But how much support would be there from the opposition, if India is likely to initiate an aggression? Second,the level of internal support is also determined by achievements on the battlefield. If the Indian offensive is productive in terms of destroying the militant camps or keeping the Pakistan army on the defensive, then the level of internal support is likely to increase. On the contrary, if an Indian offensive failed to achieve its objective in the initial days and weeks or the Indian security forces are subjected to heavy casualties, internal support is likely to diminish. In Kargil, internal support was widespread, as Indian forces were fighting to repel an invasion and against external aggression.

The second factor that would constrain an Indian limited war scenario would be the level of external support. How much external support would India be able to garner during a limited war? The first response from the international community would be that of condemning Indian actions if it violated the LoC. External pressure would be exerted in various forms. First, the international community led by the United States would pressure India to call for a ceasefire immediately and halt military operations. Major states would also send emissaries to defuse the situation and call for India to withdraw its forces to its side of the LoC. If the Kargil conflict is to be taken as an example, the international community refused to agree with Pakistan and supported India, as the invasion was perceived as a case of Pakistani aggression.

The third factor that would be the most crucial in constraining India's objectives and actions in a limited war situation would be Pakistan's response. What if Pakistan decides to expand the war? After all, why should Pakistan limit the war, if it is not in its interests? In the event of Indian limited war across the LoC opposite to either the Baramulla or Rajouri and Poonch sectors, and India is able to thrust forward, how would Pakistan respond? Would Pakistan fight only in these sectors? Will Pakistan use only its army and paramilitary forces or would it also use its air force?

During the Kargil conflict, India decided to fight on its side of the LoC, as Pakistan convinced India and the international community in the initial period that the infiltrators were only *mujahideen*. Since Pakistan never admitted the involvement of its troops and India was not certain in the initial period about the background of the infiltrators, India's efforts were mainly aimed at removing the infiltrators and not at crossing the LoC. India withstood the pressure to cross over. Will Pakistan also pursue the same strategy if India decides to execute a Kargil-like operation on the other side of the LoC?

Unlike Pakistan, India would not be able to claim that the infiltrators across the LoC are not from its armed forces. Right from day one, there would be open hostilities between Indian and Pakistani forces. Pakistan's strategy then would be aimed at removing the Indian forces from "its soil" and not removing "Indian infiltrators." Hence, it is unlikely that the Pakistani response would have the limitations that India had during the Kargil conflict.

Why would Pakistan limit its response, if an Indian limited war is not in its favor? Pakistan would be tempted to expand the war for the following reasons. First, it would increase the pressure on India politically, on whether or not it was fighting a "limited" war. Instead of responding only to the Indian infiltration in select sectors, Pakistan may attempt to increase the areas of conflict from Jammu to Kargil. How then would India respond, as the limited war is expanding? Would India stick to its original plan of a limited war in a limited area? The first reason for Pakistan to expand the war would be to increase the political pressure on India.

Second, Pakistan would be tempted to expand the limited war to increase pressure on India militarily. India then would be forced to fight all along the LoC, depending on whether Pakistan likes to expand the war only along the LoC or even along the international border in the Jammu sectors. An increased scope of military activity would deny an immediate outcome, thus negating any initial success of Indian forces in Pakistanoccupied Kashmir.

Third, Pakistan would also be tempted to expand the conflict because of internal political factors. Pakistani armed forces are well aware that any military defeat at the hands of Indian forces would be politically disastrous for its internal influence. Rather than being bogged down in a select area, Pakistan would likely confront the Indian forces, bringing about a military stalemate. The Pakistan army is also well aware that in case of an open military conflict, neither side can emerge victorious in the short run. A military stalemate at a larger level would then definitely be a better option for Pakistani forces, irrespective of high casualties, than a military defeat in a limited conflict with lesser casualties. Even an economic breakdown due to a larger conflict would be acceptable to Pakistan's military, rather than the maintenance of a stable economy in a limited conflict. What would ultimately matter for Pakistan's security forces would be its prestige and its position inside Pakistan.

Fourth, Pakistan would also be tempted to expand the conflict for external factors. Any expansion of the conflict is bound to increase the international anxiety over an Indo-Pak nuclear war. The longer and broader the conflict in terms of time and territory, the more the international community, led by the United States, is bound to increase its pressure. Any such international pressure, as seen in the previous incidents, is bound only to reassert the status quo. Pakistan's decision to expand the war would be aimed at increasing the international pressure on India to withdraw its forces to their pre-conflict positions.

If Pakistan decides to expand the conflict, how would it pursue that option? It would obviously use its air force on both sides of the LoC. Would it use nuclear weapons? As seen in the previous chapters, there have been a number of threats from Pakistan on its resolve to use nuclear weapons during a conflict. Would Pakistan really use nuclear weapons if it is facing defeat in a limited war situation?

Two important questions need to be raised in a hypothetical situation. One, what if Pakistan, facing the threat of losing a limited war, decides to use nuclear weapons against one or more targets inside India? Two, what if Pakistan, after failing to stop the Indian military offensive, decides to use nuclear weapons inside its territory, but against the advancing Indian troops?

Another important factor that could limit the initial Indian objectives of a limited war would be a militant attack in the Indian heartland. During a limited war scenario, how would India respond if there is a militant attack, either on a personality of high political value or on a symbol of what India stands for? What if the militants succeed in attacking the prime minister, home minister, or the defense minister? What if the militants succeed in carrying out another attack on the Parliament similar to the one on December 13, 2001? What if the militants succeed in carrying an attack like that of Kaluchak? Would India then still contemplate a limited conflict or would it be pressured to escalate the conflict?

To conclude, the question is whether or not there is sufficient space for India to wage a limited war with Pakistan. However, a more important query is whether or not such a limited war will secure India's interests vis-à-vis Pakistan. Irrespective of the space under the nuclear umbrella, if a limited war does not secure India's political interests, then such an option need not be pursued. On the other hand, if exercising the limited war option secures India's political interests, then India should attempt exploring such a space. Therefore, the crucial question is: would a limited war secure India's political interests vis-à-vis Pakistan in general and Jammu and Kashmir in particular?

CHAPTER FOUR
Will a Limited War Secure Indian Interests?

Looking for Objectives—Limited or Unlimited?

Any war, whether limited or not, should be based on certain objectives, which are either political or military or both. What could be India's political and military objectives in waging a limited war? By definition, limited wars are fought for political objectives, in which the armed forces are to carry out the objectives spelt out by the political leadership.[1] First, what could the political objectives of India be, if it decides to wage a limited war?[2]

It is essential to map Indian political objectives vis-à-vis Pakistan's, especially with regards to Kashmir. Any political or military strategy that the Indian government plans to undertake should be aimed at fulfilling these objectives. Any military strategy, whether limited war or unlimited war, conventional or nuclear, preemptive or surgical strikes, should then fit into a larger framework of achieving those political objectives.

Indian objectives vis-à-vis Pakistan and Kashmir, broadly classified, could be the following at national, bilateral, and international levels.

- To get back the territory that Pakistan has been occupying since the First Indo-Pak War in 1948.
- To convert the LoC into a permanent border and to force

1. Robert E. Osgood, *Limited War: The Challenge to American Strategy* (Chicago: The University of Chicago Press, 1957), 13.
2. Suba Chandran, "Limited War, Unlimited Questions," *Peace and Conflict* 6, no. 2 (2003): 5.

Pakistan consider this option as a permanent solution to the Kashmir dispute.

- To prevent Pakistan from supporting the separatist and militant movement in Jammu and Kashmir.
- To combat the militant movement in Jammu and Kashmir and prevent terrorist attacks all over India.
- To integrate the state of Jammu and Kashmir, especially the people of Kashmir, psychologically into the Indian mainstream.
- To have Pakistan as a stable democracy, where the role of the military is minimized in taking political decisions vis-à-vis India.
- To minimize external involvement in the bilateral issues between India and Pakistan.

Any Indian strategy should be aimed at fulfilling these primary objectives. Clearly any military strategy should then conform to these major political objectives. A military strategy could only be a means to achieve these political objectives, irrespective of such a strategy resulting in a gain or loss at the ground level. In other words, even if India would lose a military battle, but win the war at the political level, such a military strategy is worth pursuing, as long as the results help India to achieve its political objectives. However, a military strategy, even if it results in India winning the battle, but ultimately affects its long-term political objectives, is not worth pursuing. If political objectives are negatively affected, then any war, limited or unlimited, would prove unproductive, despite victory.

The primary issue then is not winning a battle, but the war. It is essential to analyze the concept of limited war with Pakistan in this background. Will a limited war with Pakistan secure India's interests? The primary objective of limited war with Pakistan, then, is not to focus on whether there is a space for conducting such a military strategy or whether India could win a limited war. Rather, the focus of any limited war should be aimed at whether it would secure India's interests in Jammu and Kashmir amid the larger issues of Indo-Pak relations. No less important is the issue of whether a limited war with Pakistan would secure India's stability at the national level.

It is worth analyzing what implications a limited war could have on the above-mentioned primary objectives of India.

First, would a limited war with Pakistan enable India to get back lost territories in Kashmir? According to the Parliamentary Resolution passed on February 22, 1994, the

> State of Jammu and Kashmir has been, is and shall be an integral part of India and any attempts to separate it from the rest of the country will be resisted by all necessary means...Pakistan must vacate the areas of the Indian State of Jammu and Kashmir, which they have occupied through aggression...[3]

This objective exists only at the rhetorical level. India would only be too happy if Pakistan is willing to give back those territories that it had occupied in the 1948 war. Today, except for miniscule rightist elements, no one in India, either in the government or outside it, considers getting back those lost territories "at any cost." For all practical purposes, the government and the people at large, though they may be hesitant to declare it publicly, are aware that those territories are lost forever. They have only a bargaining value for India. In fact, the Indian government is willing to convert the existing Line of Control into a permanent border.

---

3. The Parliamentary Resolution dated February 22, 1994 also states that "India has the will and capacity to firmly counter all designs against its unity, sovereignty and territorial integrity; and demands that...all attempts to interfere in the internal affairs of India will be met resolutely."

Many inside India are well aware that Pakistan would never return those occupied territories or even remove its troops from there. To a large extent, this objective has become defunct. If India has given up this objective at the political level, then the question of waging a limited war to win back those territories does not exist. Besides, even if India considers this objective seriously and pursues a military option, a limited war would simply not be sufficient. Even retired military personnel in India agree that "recapturing PoK [Pakistanoccupied Kashmir]—a parliamentary military objective—is a pipe dream, least of all when the two armies are fully deployed in battle locations and any tactical surprise is ruled out."[4]

Second, will a limited war enable India to force Pakistan to agree to convert the LoC into an international border? India would be willing to settle for this conversion as a final settlement. However, Pakistan has rejected this option. For them, the LoC is the problem. And they ask: why should we accept the problem as a solution?

Would India be able to force Pakistan through a limited war to agree to this conversion? Any armed conflict between India and Pakistan across the LoC would immediately attract international attention. The presence of nuclear weapons within India and Pakistan has forced and would force the international community in the future to freeze any armed incursions immediately. Both during the Kargil conflict and the year-long confrontation in 2002, the international community pressured both India and Pakistan to respect the LoC and reach an agreement through negotiations.

Neither Pakistan nor the international community would

4. Ashok K. Mehta, "Shifting Policies Deter Military Resolve," *The Pioneer*, January 4, 2003.

approve of Indian efforts to convert the LoC into an international border through military means. India can effectively achieve this result only through political means via negotiations.

Third, will a limited war reduce Pakistan's support for militancy in Kashmir? The proponents of the limited war thesis believe that limited war with Pakistan could be a major strategy to make Pakistan realize its folly and teach it a lesson for supporting militancy in Kashmir. According to this position, a limited war would increase the cost for Pakistan supporting militancy besides proving a point that India is sincere and earnest in tackling infiltration. It would also send signals to militant groups operating from Pakistan-occupied Kashmir that if they continue their activities there would be no safe havens, as India would be willing to target their camps.

Militancy has been used by Pakistan as a specific strategy to keep the conflict in Kashmir alive. It is highly unlikely that Pakistan would be coerced through a limited war to stop its support for militancy. Pakistan is well aware that the moment it stops supporting militancy, it would lose its leverage over Kashmir. One main reason for Pakistan initiating Kargil was to give a fillip to the declining militancy in Kashmir.

Fourth, will a limited war reduce militancy in Kashmir? If Kargil is to be taken as a limited conflict, then did it reduce militancy in Kashmir? If the argument could be widened, would a military option with Pakistan reduce militancy in Kashmir? If militant attacks could be graphed for the last decade, it would be clear that militancy in fact has increased since the Kargil conflict.

Table 4.1: Will a Limited War Secure India's Interests?

Objective	Will a Limited War Help?	Remarks/Questions
Reclaiming the territory under Pakistan's occupation	No	India would need to wage a full conventional war to reclaim the territories It is doubtful that India will be able to hold onto the territory, even if it claims it
Converting the LoC into a permanent border	Unlikely	The political costs to either the democratic polity or the military in Pakistan would be too high Pakistan would rather risk a full conventional war
Preventing Pakistan from supporting the separatist and militant movement in Jammu and Kashmir	Unlikely	Neither the failure in Kargil, nor the threat of war in 2002 prevented Pakistan from continuing its support
Combatting the militant movement in Jammu and Kashmir and preventing	Unlikely	The militant attacks would only intensify. Events surrounding the Kargil conflict and 2002 border confrontation are adequate examples

and preventing terrorist attacks all over India		
Integrating the state of Jammu and Kashmir, especially the people of Kashmir, psychologically into the Indian mainstream	Unlikely	The Kashmiris were indifferent during the Kargil conflict No support, political or popular, could be expected from Kashmir during any limited war with Pakistan
Having a stable and democratic Pakistan where the role of the military is minimized in taking political decisions vis-à-vis India	Unlikely	Any armed conflict with Pakistan would only increase the role of the military, and military expenditures would increase in Pakistan
Minimizing external involvement in bilateral issues between India and Pakistan, especially over Kashmir	Unlikely	Pakistan would only emphasize that Kashmir is an "international" issue and a "nuclear flashpoint"

Militant Attacks in Kashmir before and after Kargil Conflict

The following tables illustrate the rising frequency of militant attacks in relation to the Kargil conflict.[5]

Table 4.2: Militant Attacks on Security Forces

Year	Killed	Year	Killed
1993	216	1999	555
1994	236	2000	638
1995	297	2001	590
1996	376	2002	469
1997	355	2003	338
1998	339		

Table 4.3: Attacks on Minority Communities since 1998

District	No. of Attacks	If casualties, numbers killed in each attack	Total
Udhampur	5	9,4,5,7,8,3	36
Doda	17	26,15,20,29,13,4,5,6,5,5,15	141
Rajori	10	11,9,3,12,10,5,4	54
Poonch	4	9,5,2,6	22
Anantnag	4	15,7,13,2	37
Pahalgam	3	23,5,8	36
Jammu	4	13,30,28,13	84
Pulawama	1	24	24
Anantnag	4	15,7,13,	2 37

5. Data compiled through various sources, including reports that appeared in newspapers, South Asia Terrorism Portal (http://www.satp.org), and the Indian army's website (http://www.armyinkashmir.org).

Table 4.4: Attacks on Political Activists

Year	Killed	Year	Killed
1993	0	1999	53
1994	8	2000	30
1995	16	2001	49
1996	75	2002	87
1997	52	2003	31
1998	30		

The three tables on militant attacks above reveal that militancy in Kashmir has been revived after the Kargil conflict. In fact, the militant attacks have intensified in the form of *fidayeen* attacks. A difference needs to be made between the *fidayeen* attacks and suicide attacks, though the media and the militants refer to the *fidayeen* attacks as suicide attacks, most likely because doing so gives them more publicity.[6] *Fidayeen* attacks, however, are hit and run attempts and do not use suicide bombs. The *fidayeen* attacks are daring raids on military camps by a group of militants. They represent a post-Kargil conflict phenomenon in that they have been increasing noticeably since that time.

Table 4.5: *Fidayeen* Attacks since the Kargil Conflict

22 July 2003	A *fidayeen* squad attacked an army camp in Akhnoor, killing eight security forces including a brigadier
28 June 2003	A *fidayeen* squad attacked an army installation in Sunjwan, killing 12 soldiers

6. Suba Chandran, "Fighting the *Fidayeens*: Combating Suicide Terrorism in Kashmir," in *Terrorism Post 9/11 An Indian Perspective*, eds. P.R. Chari and Suba Chandran (New Delhi: Manohar Publishers, 2003), 136-138.

26 April 2003	A *fidayeen* squad attacked the All India Radio Station in Srinagar, killing two security forces
25 April 2003	A two-member *fidayeen* squad attacked a BSF headquarters at Madar, killing three BSF personnel
14 March 2003	A deputy superintendent of police along with three civilians were killed in Poonch
19 December 2002	One security force personnel was killed and three injured in a *fidayeen* attack at Khablan village, Thana Mandi
24 November 2002	13 civilans were killed by a two-member *fidayeen* squad in two shrines-- Raghunath and Panjbakhtar temples—in Jammu
21 September 2002	A police personnel was killed in Srinagar in a *fidayeen* attack
14 May 2002 36	persons were killed by a *fidayeen* squad in an attack on the army cantonment in Kaluchak
30 March 2002	Three security forces personnel were killed by a two-member *fidayeen* attack in Jammu
8 December 2001	A two-member *fidayeen* squad killed a security force personnel at Azad Kunj
22 October 2001	A four-member *fidayeen* squad was killed after they attacked an IAF station at Avantipur

1 October 2001	36 persons were killed in a *fidayeen* attack on the State Legislative Assembly complex
17 September 2001	A two-member *fidayeen* squad killed nine security forces personnel in Handwara
7 August 2001	Two security forces personnel and seven civilians were killed in a *fidayeen* attack at the Jammu railway station.
9 February 2001	A four-member *fidayeen* squad attacked the police control room in Srinagar
16 January 2001	Four security forces personnel were killed in a *fidayeen* attack on Srinagar Airport

The Kargil conflict has not only revived militancy in Kashmir, but has also intensified it. Will a limited war initiated by India then be able to reduce militancy in Kashmir?

Fifth, will a limited war with Pakistan result in the Kashmiris supporting the Indian side? It is unlikely. During the Kargil conflict, there was not much local support for India's war efforts in Kashmir. The Kashmiris considered the Kargil conflict as "India's War" and not theirs. The general euphoria that was found in other parts of the country was strangely lacking in the Kashmir Valley. Some of the Kashmiris were "even glad to see the Indian troops on the defensive."[7] According to a local college student in Srinagar, "It [Kargil conflict] is good, these people [Indian security forces] should know what a real war means. It is easy to stop civilian passenger

7. Muzamil Jaleel, "It Was Not Our War," in *Guns and Yellow Roses: Essays on the Kargil War* (New Delhi: Harper Collins Publishers, 1999), 65.

buses and ask us to come down and frisk and humiliate our womenfolk. Let them get a beating."[8] A section in Kashmir in fact welcomed the Kargil conflict as "the conflict brought temporary relief to a region that had been bowed under the heavy presence of Indian troops for years. Redeploying many of these troops to Kargil meant less crackdown operations, less checkpoints, and less army movements in many villages and towns."[9]

Muzamil Jaleel summed up the feeling inside Kashmir over Kargil:

> The Kargil war was fought, won and lost. Both India and Pakistan claimed victory, amid jingoism and nationalistic fervour. But in Kashmir both sides seem to have lost. The war on the barren mountains of Kargil has exposed both India and Pakistan in the Valley. For those Kashmiris who believed in "Kashmir to Kanyakumari is one," many queries arise. Why was this sympathy wave missing when Kashmiris were being killed for the past ten years? Why was there no newspaper advertisement to collect donations for victims of violence in Kashmir? Why was there no outpouring of nationalistic fervour even when fifty civilians were killed on a Srinagar street?[10]

Sixth, will a limited war reduce the influence of the military and establish a stable democracy in Pakistan? A stable and democratic Pakistan is clearly in the interests of India. A limited war, as happened in Kargil, would only strengthen the status and power of the military in Pakistan's power equations. It is evident that in any limited war scenario Pakistani forces cannot be decimated to the extent it happened during the 1971 Indo-Pak War.

In the 1971 war, the Pakistani forces faced an ignominious

---

8. A local college student in Srinagar quoted in Jaleel, "It Was Not Our War," 65.
9. Jaleel, "It Was Not Our War," 72.
10. Ibid., 93.

defeat, which witnessed them surrendering to the Indian forces; thousands of Pakistani soldiers taken as prisoners of war; and ultimately East Pakistan (Bangladesh) breaking away and emerging as an independent nation. In the immediate aftermath of the 1971 war, the armed forces of Pakistan lost their status and prestige inside Pakistan for the first time since the 1947 independence. The military's defeat at the hands of India and its inability to protect the territorial integrity of Pakistan also reduced their influence over its polity, at least for a temporary period. Zulfikar Ali Bhutto succeeded in shadowing the political power and influence of the armed forces for a couple of years. The armed forces were thoroughly demoralized and dared not influence the initial political events following the 1971 war. Had they attempted, the people of Pakistan would have risen up against their armed forces, so much was the hatred and dissatisfaction of the former towards the latter at the time.

Unless Pakistan's armed forces were defeated at that level, it is highly unlikely that they would lose their influence in national politics. Any limited war with Pakistan is unlikely to create that situation for its armed forces. On the contrary, a limited war would only strengthen the hold of the military over Pakistan's politics and society.

What if India succeeds in a limited war scenario and is able to reach the militant camps in PoK and destroy them? What if the Pakistani armed forces lose a significant area in PoK to the Indian forces in a limited war situation? Presuming that India succeeds in occupying an area, forcing hundreds of Pakistani soldiers to surrender and be taken as prisoners of war, and Pakistani forces are unable to remove the Indian forces, what are the likely outcomes? Would they secure India's security interests?

First, Pakistan would attempt to restore the status quo by forcing the Indian forces to retreat. It would concentrate mainly in those sectors that Indian troops occupy. Like India during the Kargil conflict, Pakistan is also sure to rule out any negotiations as long as Indian forces remain deployed across the LoC. Even if India is willing to negotiate a cease-fire, Pakistan would refuse that option until it is able to regain the lost positions. The people of Pakistan are sure to back such an option. In that case, the armed forces of Pakistan are bound to be portrayed by its people as the defenders of their country's territory and as heroes who withstood Indian aggression.

Another outcome also needs to be taken into account in a scenario where the Indian forces occupy a section in PoK and take considerable numbers of prisoners of war. What if the fundamentalist forces, including *jihadi* groups, take over Pakistan's polity? Can such a situation be completely ruled out? With the armed forces defeated and the secular democratic forces not able to recoup, the possibility of fundamentalist forces filling the power vacuum remains.

The religious parties have succeeded in filling up the vacuum created by the poor performance of moderate parties in Baluchistan and the North West Frontier Province. While the religious parties never had much influence in the main province—Punjab—*jihadi* and sectarian forces mainly emanate from there. If the *jihadi* forces and the religious parties come together overtly, such an alliance would pose a serious threat to Pakistan in a crisis situation in which the Pakistani forces are bogged down along the border.

In either of these cases, even India winning a limited conflict would not serve its security interests in the long run. In the first scenario, which is most likely, the popular support for the armed forces inside Pakistan is bound to be reinforced and increased. In the second case, though unlikely, Pakistan is bound to become an unstable and fundamentalist country, which then would become an epicenter of *jihad*, exporting its brand of Islam. In such an event, the initial Indian objective of attacking militant camps through a limited war would only backfire.

Clearly, irrespective of the existence of a political space to conduct a limited war, any such military adventure would not achieve much in support of India's interests. A limited war would not bring the PoK back to the Indian fold; a limited war would not force Pakistan to agree to convert the LoC into an international border; a limited war would not prevent militancy in Jammu and Kashmir; a limited war would not remove the alienation inside Kashmir and integrate the population into the mainstream; a limited war would not undermine the influence of the military in Pakistani politics; and a limited war would not bring any international support for India's stand on Kashmir.

Is There an Alternative Strategy to Secure Indian Interests?

If limited war will not achieve India's interests, then is there an alternative strategy that would achieve India's interests in Kashmir? As seen in the second chapter, limited war arose in India as an alternative strategy because earlier attempts failed to achieve anything substantial.

India's strategies all along have been to reach an understanding on Kashmir at the New Delhi-Islamabad level. What India has failed to understand is that since the 1980s, a majority of Kashmiris are not supportive of India and there does exist alienation and a sense of deprivation—both actual and imagined—amongst the Kashmiris. Bad governance and narrow politics by successive governments have completely distanced Srinagar from New Delhi. Islamabad has been successful in exploiting this distance between New Delhi and Srinagar, particularly concentrating on the political frustration amongst Kashmiris and the continuous bad governance of the state. Had it not been for bad governance, alienation, and deteriorating New Delhi-Srinagar relations, Pakistan would have never succeeded in abetting militancy in Jammu and Kashmir. New Delhi provided the causes and Islamabad only exploited them.

If India is to address Pakistan, then it has to be based on a long-term strategy aimed at improving the relations between New Delhi and Srinagar; providing better governance; and removing the feeling of alienation amongst the Kashmiris. The road to Islamabad for New Delhi runs through Srinagar, and unless the ride is smooth, India will never be able to reach Pakistan.

An improved New Delhi-Srinagar relationship would considerably reduce the level of militancy in Jammu and Kashmir. In the long run, positive relations can undermine conditions that foster militancy, as happened in Punjab. At least the situation could be brought back to its pre-1987 level. Once the level of militancy is reduced and relations between Srinagar and New Delhi improve, Pakistan's hold over Kashmir would start withering away. Obviously, there would still be a group inside Jammu and Kashmir demanding independence or who may owe allegiance to Pakistan, but they would not have any real support at the ground level. Pakistan would still talk about its "political" support to the freedom movement in Kashmir, but there would be no takers in Kashmir or for that matter even inside Pakistan.

Political leadership inside Kashmir, both moderate and separatist, is aware that an independent Kashmir is nothing but a dream. Abdul Ghani Bhat, former Chairman of the Hurriyat Conference, said in a 2003 interview:

> In my honest view, independent Kashmir is not a workable idea. Indians don't accept it, Pakistanis too more importantly. China may also not choose to accept it. The reasons are not far to seek, and are as obvious as anything. Maybe all three do not accept it and therefore, Kashmir doesn't go independent.[11]

Most of the Kashmiris, especially in rural areas, demand employment, electricity, water, and freedom from harassment by the security forces. A*zadi* (independence) as a demand comes in only fifth in the ranking of concerns for people in rural areas. The *azadi* demand comes first, with the rest later, only among the people of Srinagar.

In the recent past, New Delhi has taken considerable steps, which need to be further strengthened. For the first time in decades, New Delhi succeeded in organizing free and fair elections for the legislative assembly of Jammu and Kashmir. While there have been minor criticisms of the elections held in 2002, they were accepted as free and fair by most inside and outside India. The Peoples Democratic Party (PDP) formed a government with support from the Congress Party and other parties. The government led by the PDP is seen as independent by many inside Kashmir, as for the first time the state is being ruled by a non-National Conference (NC) government. The NC has always been seen as the stooge of the Union government.

Second, Vajpayee addressed the Kashmiris and initiated a new process in April 2003 to build the relationship between New Delhi and Srinagar. N.N. Vohra has been appointed as

---

11 Amin Masoodi, "We Will Contribute to the Peace Process: Abdul Ghani Bhat," Institute of Peace and Conflict Studies (IPCS), article no. 1080 (July 7, 2003), http://www.ipcs.org/ipcs/new/newKashmirLevel2.jsp?action=showView&kValue=1090&subCatID=null&mod=null.

the Union government's chief interlocutor to speak to Kashmiris. Though many Kashmiris are critical about Vohra's initiative, the response to it has been positive in terms of conveying what the Kashmiris want.[12]

Third, New Delhi has also initiated a dialogue at the highest level between the separatist groups—led by the Hurriyat and the Union home minister. The first round of talks took place in February 2004 and the second round in April 2004.

Fourth, India has also initiated a new dialogue process with Pakistan starting in October 2003. The Islamabad summit and the follow-up joint statement between Vajpayee and Musharraf initiated a new process at the bilateral level between India and Pakistan.

Fifth, there seems to be an open rift between the militant groups and their erstwhile masters—a section inside the Pakistani army. The militant and *jihadi* groups seem to have become independent and are even retaliating against the Pakistani army. Two assassination attempts were made on General Musharraf in December 2003.

New Delhi should recognize these changing conditions and initiate a new process aimed at bringing the Kashmiris closer to the Indian mainstream.

First, it is imperative that New Delhi devolves an element

---

12. Amin Masoodi, "Popular Perception of the Kashmir Conflict: Srinagar Round," IPCS, article no. 1040 (May 26, 2003), http://www.ipcs.org/ipcs/new/newKashmirLevel2.jsp?action=showView&kValue=1048 & subCatID=null&mod =null, and Amin Masoodi, "Popular Perception of the Kashmir Conflict: Kupwara, Handwara and Sopore Round," IPCS, article no. 1055 (June 24, 2003), http://www.ipcs.org/ipcs/new/new Kashmir Leve 12. jsp ? action=showView &k Value = 1070 & sub Cat ID = null & mod = null.

of autonomy to Jammu and Kashmir. For example, New Delhi could change the nomenclature of the head of the state to *Wazir-e-Azam* and *Sadar-i-Riyasat* for State Executive. The state of Jammu and Kashmir could be provided a significant role in selecting its governor. According to the Independent Study Team for the Delhi Policy Group:

> The Governor could be elected by the State legislature and appointed by the President and by virtue of Article 156 (1) hold office at the pleasure of the President; or the State government could submit a panel of names and the President would appoint as Governor the person he finds most suitable from the panel, and he would hold office at the President's pleasure; or the President would submit a name which the legislature might endorse. The President could then appoint the governor and the latter would hold office at his pleasure.[13]

Second, India needs to improve its human rights record and also dispel some myths regarding human rights violations. Many inside Kashmir support militancy due to the harassment from security forces. While an element of human rights violations is sometimes unavoidable in a conflict situation, the fact that Indian forces could improve their track record is undeniable. Though there is no need for an external monitoring of human rights conditions in Jammu and Kashmir, the National Human Rights Commission (NHRC) should be given full powers to monitor the situation.[14]

---

13. Kanti Bajpai, Dipankar Banerjee, and Amitabh Mattoo, *Jammu and Kashmir: An Agenda for the Future,* Report of the Independent Study Team for the Delhi Policy Group, January 1998, 7.
14. There have been many calls for an independent human rights monitor in Kashmir. The argument is that the "independent monitoring of human rights violations serves the national interests best, prevents further alienation of the people, prevents defaming of India abroad and helps in improving the discipline of the security forces." See Balraj Puri, "Kashmir Problem Thrives on Denial of Human and Democratic Rights," *Economic and Political Weekly,* August 3, 1999, 795.

Third, India could constitute a commission on the disappeared. It has been reported by Mushtaq Ahmad Lone, former home minister of Jammu and Kashmir in the state legislative assembly in 1999, that the government is aware of 3,257 people who have gone missing ever since the violence escalated in Kashmir.[15] Current chief minister of the state, Mufti Mohammad Sayeed, also reported in the state legislative assembly that, 741 have disappeared since 2000.[16] Independent accounts estimate that the figure could be as high as 6,000.[17]

A committee on disappearances on the models of Truth and Reconcilation Committees of South Africa would go a long way in redefining the faith of people in government institutions. Such a commission would also prove to be beneficial to the state in addressing many false accusations of these disappearances.

Fourth, India should take adequate measures to address the conditions of the victims of the conflicts, especially that of widows, "half-widows," and orphans. According to independent estimates, there are roughly around 10,000 to 50,000 widows in the Valley.[18] Besides the widows, there are a number of "half widows" in the Valley, whose husbands have either crossed over to Pakistan or were killed by the security forces, but their identity has not been established or they have simply disappeared. Besides widows and half widows, according to independent estimates there are around 35,000-

15. Gautam Navlakha, "Internal War and Civil Rights: Disappearances in Jammu and Kashmir," *Economic and Political Weekly*, June 12, 1999.
16. *The Asian Age*, April 18, 2003.
17. "Kashmir Assembly Election: How Free and Fair," *Economic and Political Weekly*, January 11, 2003, 101.
18. There were roughly 10,000 widows in 1999 (see Muzamil Jaleel, "Wounds of Valley's Widows Fester," *The Indian Express*, May 11, 1999) and more than 54,000 widows in 2001 (see *Reshaping the Agenda in Kashmir*, International Center for Peace Initiatives, 2002, 3).

40,000 orphans in Kashmir.[19]

Fifth, the Union government should initiate a serious dialogue with the entire spectrum of Kashmiris, including that of the Hurriyat Conference. A dialogue with the Hurriyat is essential because it occupies a certain political space, minimizing the space for the militants.

> A marginalized and divided Hurriyat will not be in the interest of India, at least, until the democratic process in the Valley is re-established. Such a marginalization of the Hurriyat would in effect reduce the significant political space that presently it is occupying, and would increase the space for militancy. In fact the Hurriyat to an extent has been resisting the space for the militants. It has been against the militants calling for hartals. In fact, to an extent the hartals organized by the Hurriyat have been acting as a vent for the public in Kashmir to express their dissatisfaction and anger against the government. To an extent, the Hurriyat act as the safety-valve and it is in the government's interest that the Hurriyat continue to occupy this space.[20]

India's efforts in Jammu and Kashmir thus should be aimed at reducing the space between New Delhi and Srinagar. Such an effort would automatically also reduce Pakistan's space in Jammu and Kashmir. In such an eventuality Pakistan would have two options. First, it could attempt to increase the level of militancy in the Kashmir valley, thereby negating any advantage that India might accrue due to the reduced space between New Delhi and Srinagar. Or Pakistan could attempt to reach a political compromise with India, before it loses all its leverage vis-à-vis Jammu and Kashmir. While the Indian security forces have the ability to meet the situation if Pakistan

---

19. Quoted in "Kashmir Assembly Election: How Free and Fair," *Economic and Political Weekly*, January 11, 2003, 101.
20. Suba Chandran, *India's Security Problematique* (forthcoming).

decides to opt for the first option, India would have no problem in politically engaging Pakistan if the latter decides to pursue the second option.

To conclude, what is essential for India is to win the political objectives vis-à-vis Kashmir and Pakistan. Any military strategy should be aimed at fulfilling these political objectives. If a given military strategy, irrespective of winning or losing, is to result in India achieving these political objectives, then such an option is worth pursuing. In fact, India should carry out a military option in that case. On the contrary, if a military strategy will backfire on India's long-term political objectives, irrespective of India gaining at the battleground militarily, then such an option is not worth pursuing.

Limited war as a military option is unlikely to gain any significant political objectives in the present situation. In that case, irrespective of the political space needed to conduct a limited war and irrespective of India making gains in the battle, it may not secure India's long-term security interests. The primary question then should not be whether or not there exists a space to conduct a limited war under a nuclear umbrella; rather, it should be whether a limited war would secure India's interests in Kashmir and vis-à-vis Pakistan. Clearly, India should aim at winning the war at the political level and not the battle at the military level.

Select Bibliography

"52 Militants Died in Kargil Operation," *The Indian Express*, May 19, 1999.
"Aircrafts Were within LoC," *The Hindu*, May 29, 1999
"Ammunition over, Infiltrators on the Run, Claims Army," *The Indian Express*, May 24, 1999.
"Anza Missiles Used to Down Indian Jets," *The News*, May 28, 1999.
"Anza Missiles Used to Down Indian Jets," *The News*, May 28, 1999.
"Armies Establish Contact on Hotline," *The Times of India*, May 27, 1999.
"Armies Establish Contact on Hotline," *The Times of India*, May 27, 1999.
"Arms Dump Blown up in Shelling in Kargil," *Daily Excelsior*, May 10, 1999.
"Army Closing in on Infiltrators," *The Hindu*, May 24, 1999.
"Army Reaches LoC in Batalik," *The Hindu*, July 10, 1999.
"Army Recaptures Point 5140," *The Pioneer*, June 21, 1999.
"Army Recovers Gas Masks from Pak Soldier," *The Times of India*, June 15, 1999.
"Army Recovers Last Major Peak," *The Indian Express*, July 11, 1999.
"Back-channel Diplomacy," *The Indian Express*, July 1, 1999.
"Bin Laden Worked in Tandem with Pak to Push Infiltrators," *Hindustan Times*, June 15, 1999.
"Cease-fire Only after Infiltrators Quit: Fernandes," *The Hindu*, June 2, 1999.
"Cease-fire Only after Infiltrators Quit: Fernandes," *The Hindu*, June 2, 1999.
"Centre Invites Militants, Hurriyat for Dialogue on Kashmir," *Daily Excelsior*, April 6, 2000.
"CIA's Missing Afghan Stingers Land in Kargil," *The Indian Express*, June 7, 1999.
'Clear Proof' of Pak Role," *The Hindu*, June 6, 1999.
"Coolie Killed, Three Injured in Kargil Shelling," *Daily Excelsior*, May 11, 1999.
"Crying Nuclear Wolf," *The Times of India*, June 2, 1999.
"Economy Robust Enough to Bear Kargil Cost: FM," *Hindustan Times*, June 15, 1999.
"Eviction Difficult, Admits Army," *The Times of India*, May 26, 1999.
"Eviction of Intruders Complete: DGMO," *The Hindu*, July 27, 1999.
"Fernandes Unveils 'Limited War' Doctrine," *The Hindu*, January 25, 2000.
"Fernandes Unveils 'Limited War' Doctrine," *The Hindu*, January 25, 2000.
"Fernandes, Army Chief visit battle front," *The Hindu*, 31 May 1999
"Forces Well Prepared: George," *Daily Excelsior*, May 15, 1999.
"Foreign Mercenaries Hijack J&K Secessionism," *Hindustan Times*, September 17, 1998;
"George Meets Oppn Leaders, Heads of US, UK Missions," *The Indian Express*, May 27, 1999.
"German Intelligence Says Osama Is Involved in Kashmir Crisis," *The Asian Age*, June 16, 1999.
"Govt. Blames Pak., Open for Talks," *The Hindu*, August 9, 2000.

"Heavy Casualties Feared in Kargil Operation: Hospital, Civilian Population Evacuated," *Daily Excelsior*, May 13, 1999.
"Hizbul Announces Cease-fire," *The Hindu*, July 25, 2000.
"Hizbul Chied Endorses Ceasefire," *Hindustan Times*, July 26, 2000.
"Hizbul Mujahideen Revokes Ceasefire," *The Hindu*, August 9, 2000.
"IAF Begins Round-the-clock Operations against Intruders," *The Hindu*, June 28, 1999.
"IAF Bombs Militant Posts," *The Hindu*, May 27, 1999.
"IAF Copter Shot Down," *The Hindu*, May 29, 1999.
"IAF Drops Napalm on Hideouts," *The Pioneer*, May 3, 1999.
"IAF Hits Enemy Supply Base," *The Hindu*, June 18, 1999
"IAF Jets Pound Tiger Hills," *The Hindu*, June 25, 1999
"IAF Laser Bombs Zero in on Camps," *The Asian Age*, June 27, 1999.
"IAF Loses Two Aircraft in Action," *The Hindu*, May 28, 1999
"IAF Pounding of Enemy on Top of Tiger Hill Continues," *Hindustan Times*, June 26, 1999
"IAF Squadrons on Alert as Kargil Face-off Continues," *The Times of India*, May 21, 1999.
"IAF Strikes Supply Base in Batalik," *The Hindu*, June 27, 1999
"India Dismisses Chances of War with Pak," *The Hindu*, June 7, 1999.
"India May Have to Cross LoC: Experts," *Hindustan Times*, June 21, 1999.
"India on 'Warpath', Accuses Pakistan," *The Times of India*, June 8, 1999.
"Indian Action Unwarranted, Says Pak," *The Hindu*, May 27, 1999.
"Indian Army Foils Pak's Game Plan," *The Hindu*, June 13, 1999.
"Indian Posts Safe: Defence Ministry," *The Hindu*, May 15, 1999.
"Indian Troops Recapture Batalik Top," *The Indian Express*, May 12, 1999.
"Indo-Pak Duel at UN over Kargil," *The Pioneer*, June 6, 1999.
"Infiltration Must End to Avoid War: Powell Sees a Way out of Crisis," *Dawn*, June 1, 2002
"Infiltration Will Be Pushed out in 48 Hours: George," *Daily Excelsior*, May 17, 1999.
"Intrusion Obviously Had Full Backing of Pak Govt.: India," *Hindustan Times*, May 27, 1999.
"Jubar Height Recaptured," *The Hindu*, July 8, 1999.
"June 7 'Not Convenient' for Talks," *The Hindu*, June 6, 1999.
"Kargil Crisis to Hit Indian Economy," *Hindustan Times*, June 22, 1999.
"Kargil Shelled Again by Pak Rangers," *The Hindu*, May 10, 1999.
"Kargil Wholly Pak Army's Deed: Gen Malik," *The Times of India*, July 19, 1999.
"Kashmir Conflict Costs India $4 Million a Day," *The Asian Age*, June 16, 1999.
"Kashmir Takes a Step towards Industrial Revival," *The Economic Times*, October 5, 1998
"Lashkar Conducted High-altitude Training for Infiltrators," *The Hindu*, June 8, 1999.
"LoC Is 'Fully' Settled," *The Hindu*, June 5, 1999.
"LoC Turns into Battlefield: 200 Pakistani Militants Storm into Kargil," *Daily*

Excelsior, May 12, 1999.
"Local Support to J&K Ultras at an All-time Low," *The Hindu*, October 6, 1998
"Malik Sees Trouble on Pak Front," *The Times of India*, May 3, 1999 .
"Mi-17 Modified for Strike Operations," *The Times of India*, May 29, 1999.
"Military Action, if Diplomatic Efforts Fail: Fernandes," *The Asian Age*, January 3, 2002.
"Most Intruders Are Pak Regulars," *The Statesman*, June 8, 1999.
"Mujahideens in Kargil Safe: Tehrik-e-Jihad," *The News*, May 27, 1999.
"Nation Must Know," *Hindustan Times*, July 2, 1999.
"Nawaz Offers to Send Sartaj Aziz to New Delhi," *The News*, May 29, 1999.
"No Role for Pakistan: PM," *The Hindu*, August 7, 2000.
"One IAF Pilot in Pak Custody," *The Hindu*, May 29, 1999
"Pak Based Militant Outfit Men in Kargil," *The Hindu*, May 24, 1999.
"Pak Hand Visible in Kashmir Insurgency," *The Hindu*, July 15, 1998.
"Pak Intruders Had Chemical Weapons: Army," *The Times of India*, July 19, 1999.
"Pak Ready for Talks Any Time: Sartaj Aziz," *The Asian Age*, June 8, 1999.
"Pak Troops Believed Engaged in Battle: Army Confirms Seventeen Casualties in Kargil," *Daily Excelsior*, May 14, 1999.
"Pak Troops Planning Airdrop in Ladakh?" *The Indian Express*, June 10, 1999.
"Pakistan Army Captures 20 Indian Posts," *The News*, May 17, 1999.
"Pakistan Calls for UN Intervention," *The News*, May 29, 1999.
"Pakistan crossed LOC, says U.N. chief," *The Hindu*, 31 May 1999
"Pakistan Intrusion in Kargil at Brigade-level," *The Indian Express*, June 26, 1999.
"Pakistan May Use Any Weapons: Shamshad," *The News*, May 31, 1999.
"Pakistan Reserves Right to Retaliate: Foreign Office," *The News*, May 27, 1999.
"Pakistan Reserves the Right to Retaliate," *The News*, May 27, 1999.
"Pakistan Sends Indian Shell for Chemical Tests," *The Times of India*, June 15, 1999.
"Pakistan Warns India," *The Statesman*, May 27, 1999.
"Pakistani Cites Nuclear Advance," *The New York Times*, February 10, 1984.
"Plan to Help Kashmir Pandits Return to the Valley," *The Statesman*, December 26, 1998.
"PM Speaks to Sharif, Says India Won't Allow Infiltration," *Daily Excelsior*, May 26, 1999.
"PM, COAS Discuss Indian Build-up at LoC," *The News*, May 23, 1999.
"Powell Expects Musharraf to Act More against Terrorists," *Hindustan Times*, January 5, 2002
"Quick Strike on the Camps across LoC is the Only Answer," *The Asian Age*, June 15, 1999.
"Rs 600 Crore More for Defence," *The Times of India*, June 14, 1999.
"Salahuddin Sets August 8 as Deadline for Tripartite Talks," *The Hindu*, August 4, 2000.
"Sartaj for UN Special Representative in Kashmir," *The News*, May 28, 1999.
"Sharif Warns of More Kargil-like Situations," *The Times of India*, June 21, 1999.
"Sharif Warns of More Kargil-like Situations," *The Times of India*, June 21, 1999.
"Stalemate in Indo-Pak Talks," *The Hindu*, June 13, 1999.

"The Action Theatre," *India Today* 24, no. 30 (July 26, 1999)
"Three Pak Battalions Active in Kargil Hills," *The Asian Age*, June 16, 1999.
"Troops Capture 6 More Heights," *The Pioneer*, June 24, 1999.
"Turnaround in J&K," *The Pioneer*, August 11, 1998
"Unified Hqrs Review Security Situation," *Daily Excelsior*, May 22, 1999.
"US Envoy Tells Pakistan to Stop Infiltration," *The News*, January 24, 2003.
"US Expects Pak to Take More Actions against Terrorists," *The Hindu*, January 6, 2002.
"War Inevitable if Diplomacy Fails, Warns Pakistan," *The Times of India*, June 15, 1999.
"War-like Situation in Kargil," *The Hindu*, May 14, 1999.
"We Can Cross the LoC, if Needed," *The Hindu*, June 24, 1999.
"We Must Not Climb Down," *The Indian Express*, January 6, 2002.
"Why Pakistan Wants the Bomb: Indian and Pakistani Perceptions," *Strategic Digest*, Vol. XV, no.10, October 1985.
"Win the Peace," *The Pioneer*, July 6, 1999.
"Withdraw Troops, PM Tells Pak.," *The Hindu*, June 15, 1999.
" M.J. Akbar, "Nawaz Sharif's Second Peace Trap," *The Asian Age*, July 4, 1999.
Ahmed, Firdaus, "The Impetus behind Limited War," *Peace and Conflict* 6, no. 2 (2003): 5.
Akbar, MJ., "The blind hawks of the BJP," *The Asian Age*, 30 May 1999
Alam, Imtiaz, "When Words Matter," *The News*, September 24, 1999.
Amit Baruah, "The Plan That Failed," *The Hindu*, July 28, 1999.
Aneja, Atul, "Kargil Conflict: Bid to Separate Ladakh", *Journal of Peace Studies*, Vol. 6, No.3, May-June,1999.
Aneja, Atul, "Pakistan Had Three-phased Plan?" *The Hindu*, June 23, 1999.
Ashok K. Mehta, "Shifting Policies Deter Military Resolve," *The Pioneer*, January 4, 2003.
Bader, William B., *The United States and the Spread of Nuclear Weapons* (New York: Pegasus, 1968)
Bajpai, Kanti et al., *Brasstacks and Beyond: Perception and Management of Crisis in South Asia* (New Delhi: Manohar Publishers, 1995), 9-12.
Bajpai, Kanti, "India's Nuclear Posture after Pokhran II," *International Studies*, Vol.37, no.4, October-December 2000.
Bajpai, Kanti, "Secure without Bomb," *Seminar*, August 1996.
Bajpai, Kanti, "The Fallacy of Indian Deterrent," in India's *Nuclear Deterrent: Pokhran II and Beyond*, ed. Amitabh Mattoo (New Delhi: Har Anand Publications, 1999)
Bajpai, Kanti, Dipankar Banerjee, and Amitabh Mattoo, *Jammu and Kashmir: An Agenda for the Future*, Report of the Independent Study Team for the Delhi Policy Group, January 1998,
Balachandran, G, "India's Nucelar Option: Economic Implications," *Strategic Analysis*, Vol.19, no.2, May 1996.
Banerjee, Dipankar, "The New Strategic Environment," in *India's Nuclear Deterrent: Pokhran II and Beyond*, ed. Amitabh Mattoo (New Delhi: Har Anand Publications,

1999)

Banerjee, Sumanta, "From Self-determination to Self-destruction", *Economic and Political Weekly*, Vol. XXXV, No.21-22, May 27,2000.

Banerjee, Sumanta, "Agra vs Kashmir", *Economic and Political Weekly*, Vol. XXXVI, No.32, August 11,2001.

Banerjee, Sumanta, "Indo-Pak Brinkmanship: At the End, What Are We Left with?", *Economic and Political Weekly*, Vol. XXXVII, No.26, June 29, 2002.

Basrur, Rajesh M, "Enduring Contradiction: Deterrence Theory and Draft Nuclear Doctrine", *Economic and Political Weekly*, Vol. XXXV, No.8-9, February 6,2000.

Baweja, Harinder and Ramesh Vinayak, "Peak by Peak," *India Today* 24, no. 24 (June 14, 1999)

Baweja, Harinder, "Slow, but Steady," *India Today* 24, no. 26 (June 28, 1999)

Bedi, Rahul, "Kargil Report: More Questions Raised Than Answered", *Economic and Political Weekly*, Vol. XXXV, No.17, April 22, 2000

Beg, Gen. Mirza Aslam, "Kargil Conflict and beyond," *The Frontier Post*, June 5, 1999

Behuria, Ashok K., "Operation Kargil: The Pakistani Popular Reactions", *Journal of Peace Studies*, Vol. 6, No.3, May-June, 1999.

Benjamin, Milton R., "India Said to Eye Raid on Pakistan's A-plants," *The Washington Post*, December 20, 1982.

Bloeria, Sudhir S., "Kargil: A Window of Opportunity" *Faultlines*, Vol.4.

Bond, Brian, *Liddell Hart: A Study of His Military Thought* (New Brunswick, NJ: Rutgers University Press, 1977)

Bowen, Clayton P. and Daniel Wolven, "Command and Control Challenges in South Asia," *The Nonproliferation Review* (spring-summer 1999): 25-35

Brodie, Bernard, "Some Notes on the Evolution of Air Doctrine," *World Politics* 7, no. 3 (April 1955).

Brodie, Bernard, "Unlimited Weapons and Limited War," *The Reporter* 11, no. 9 (November 18, 1954)

Brodie, Bernard, *Strategy in the Missile Age* (Princeton, NJ: Princeton University Press, 1959);

Carranza, Mario E., "At the Crossroads: US Non-proliferation Policy Towards South Asia After the Indian and Pakistani Tests", *Contemporary Security Policy*, Vol.23, No. 1, April 2002.

Carranza, Mario E., "An Impossible Game: Stable Nuclear Deterrence after the Indian and Pakistani Tests," *Nonproliferation Review* (spring-summer 1999).

Chandran, Suba, "Fighting the Fidayeens: Combating Suicide Terrorism in Kashmir," in *Terrorism Post 9/11: An Indian Perspective*, eds. P.R. Chari and Suba Chandran (New Delhi: Manohar Publishers, 2003)

Chandran, Suba, "Limited War, Unlimited Questions," *Peace and Conflict* 6, no. 2 (2003).

Chandran, Suba, "Why Kargil: Pakistan's Objectives and Motivations," in *Kargil: The Tables Turned*, eds. Maj. Gen. Krishna and P.R. Chari (New Delhi: Manohar Publishers, 2001)

Chari P.R., Pervaiz Iqbal Cheema, and Stephen Philip Cohen, *Perception, Politics and Security in South Asia: The Compound Crisis of 1990* (New York: RoutledgeCurzon, 2003)

Chari, PR, Pervaiz Iqbal Cheema and Ifterkharuzzaman, eds., *Nuclear Non-Proliferation in India and Pakistan* (New Delhi: Manohar Publishers, 1996)

Chari, PR., "India's Nuclear Option: Future Directions," in PR Chari et al., eds., *Nuclear Non-Proliferation in India and Pakistan* (New Delhi: Manohar Publishers, 1996)

Chari, PR., *Indo-Pak Nuclear Standoff: The Role of the United States* (New Delhi: Manohar Publishers, 1995)

Cheema, Pervaiz Iqbal, "Pakistan's Nuclear Dilemma," *Strategic Digest*, Vol.20, no.4, April 1990.

Cheema, Zafar Iqbal, "Pakistan's Nuclear Policies: Attitudes and Posture," in PR Chari et al., eds., *Nuclear Non-Proliferation in India and Pakistan* (New Delhi: Manohar Publishers, 1996)

Cheema, Zafar Iqbal, "Pakistan's Nuclear Use Doctrine and Command and Control," in Peter Lavoy, Scott Sagan and James Wirtz, ed., *Planning the Unthinkable: How New Powers will use Nuclear, Biological and Chemical Weapons* (Ithaca: Cornell University Press, 2000)

Chengappa, Raj, Saran, Rohit, and Baweja, Harinder, "Will the War Spread?" *India Today* Vol., no.27, July 5, 1999.

Chengappa, Raj, *Weapons of Peace: The Secret Story of India's Quest to be a Nuclear Power* (New Delhi: Harper Collins Publishers, 2000)

Choudhury, Kushanava, "After the Lahore Summit: The Real Story," http://www.rediff.com/news/2000/nov/23naik.htm.

Claiborne, William, "India Denies Plan to Hit Pakistani Nuclear Plants," *The Washington Post*, December 21, 1982.

Clausewitz, Karl von, *On War*, translated by O.J. Matthijs Jolles (New York: The Modern Library, 1943).

Davis, Anthony, "India woos Afghanistan at Pakistan's expanse", *Jane's Intelligence Review*, Vol.14, No.11, November 2002.

Deitchman, Seymour J., *Limited War and American Defense Policy* (Cambridge, MA: The MIT Press, 1964)

Deshpande, Anirudh, "Options in Kargil: Half-Forward Policy", *Economic and Political Weekly*, Vol. XXXIV, No.29, July 17,1999.

Deshpande, J V, "After the Conflict: Focus on Kashmir", *Economic and Political Weekly*, Vol. XXXIV, No.29, July 17,1999.

Dhamija, Sumant, "Pakistan's Cowardly Acts of Terrorism: What India Should Do", *Indian Defence Review*, Vol.16, No.4, October/December 2001.

Dhar, AK, "Pak gave Stingers to mercenaries," *The Asian Age*, 31 May 1999

Dixit, J.N., "Invasion of Kargil," *Hindustan Times*, June 23, 1999.

Dubey Muchkund, "Kargil & the Limits of Diplomacy," *The Hindu*, July 5, 1999.

Dunn, Lewis A., *Containing Nuclear Proliferation*, Adelphi Paper 263 (London: IISS, 1991)

Editorial, "Clear Line," *The Times of India*, June 5, 1999

Editorial, "Crossing the Line," *Hindustan Times*, June 25, 1999.

Editorial, "Keep Pushing ahead," *The Hindu*, June 16, 1999
Editorial, "Swearing by LoC," *Hindustan Times*, June 22, 1999.
Editorial, "The Only Choice," *Hindustan Times*, June 14, 1999.
Evans, Alexander, "India, Pakistan, and the Prospect of War," *Current History*, Vol.101, No. 654, April 2002.
Fernandes, George, "The Dynamics of Limited War," *Strategic Affairs* (October 16, 2000), http://www.stratmag.com/ issueOct-15/page07.htm.
Gacek, Christopher M., *The Logic of Force: The Dilemma of Limited War in American Foreign Policy* (New York: Columbia University Press, 1994), 16.
Garnett, John, "Limited War," in *Contemporary Strategy: Theory and Practice*, eds. John Baylis et al. (New York: Holmes & Meier Publishers, 1975), 115.
Goldenberg, Suzanne, "Early Deal to End Kashmir Conflict Was Ignored," *The Guardian*, July 22, 1999.
Hagerty, Devin T., *The Consequences of Nuclear Proliferation: Lessons from South Asia* (London: BCSIA Studies in International Security, 1998)
Halperin, Morton H., *Limited War in the Nuclear Age* (New York: John Wiley & Sons, Inc., 1963.
Haqani, Husain, "War Clouds and Pakistan's Shadow," *The Indian Express*, January 3, 2003.
Hart, B.H. Liddell, *The Revolution in Warfare* (New Haven, CT: Yale University Press, 1947).
Hazarika, Sanjoy, "The LoC Is a Border, and India Will Control It," *The Asian Age*, June 19, 1999
Hersh, Seymour, "On the Nuclear Edge," *New Yorker*, March 29, 1993
House, Karen Elliott and Peter R. Kann, "Amid a Host of Problems, Indira Gandhi Remains Serene about the State of India," *The Wall Street Journal*, July 5, 1984.
House, Karen Elliott and Peter R. Kann, "Zia Says Pakistan Has No Plans for Nuclear Bomb," *The Wall Street Journal*, July 10, 1984.
IDR Research Team, "Op Topac: The Kashmir Imbroglio," *Indian Defence Review*, April-June 99, Vol. 14. (2).
Jaleel, Muzamil, "It Was Not Our War," in *Guns and Yellow Roses: Essays on the Kargil War* (New Delhi: Harper Collins Publishers, 1999)
Jaleel, Muzamil, "Wounds of Valley's Widows Fester," *The Indian Express*, May 11, 1999
Jasjit Singh, "Budgeting for Security Needs," *Frontline* 15, no. 15 (July 31, 1998).
Jha, Prem Shankar, "Kashmir Then and Now," *The Hindu*, July 24, 1998.
John, Wilson, "Enough, Now Teach them a Lesson," *The Pioneer*, June 11, 1999.
Jones, Gregory S., "From Testing to Deploying Nuclear Forces: The Hard Choices Facing India and Pakistan," RAND Issue Paper IP-192 (2000).
Jones, Rodney W., "Pakistan's Nuclear Posture: Quest for Assured Nuclear Deterrence-A Conjecture", *Regional Studies*, Vol.XVIII, no.2.
Joshi, Akshay, "Information Warfare in Kargil," *Indian Defence Review*, April-June 99, Vol. 14
Kanet, Roger E. and Kolodziej, Edward A., eds.,*The Cold War as Cooperation: Superpower Cooperation in Regional Conflict Management* (London: Macmillan, 1991)

Kanwal, Gurmeet "Does India Need Tactical Nuclear Weapons? *Strategic Analysis*, May 2000 Vol. XXIV, no. 2.

Kanwal, Gurmeet "Implementation of India's 'No First Use' Doctrine-Need for some Inescapable Qualifications, *Strategic Analysis*, April 2000, Vol. XXIV NO.1

Kanwal, Gurmeet, "Command and Control of Nuclear Weapons in India", *Strategic Analysis*, January 2000, Vol. XXIII, no. 10.

Kanwal, Gurmeet, "India's Nuclear Doctrine and Policy", *Strategic Analysis*, Feb.2001, Vol. XXIV, no.11.

Kanwal, Gurmeet, "Nuclear Targetting Philosophy for India", *Strategic Analysis*, Vol.XXIV, No.3, June 2000.

Kargil Review Committee Report, *From Surprise to Reckoning* (New Delhi: Sage Publications, 2000).

Karim, Maj. Gen. Afsir, "Confrontation in Kargil," *Indian Defence Review*, April-June 99, Vol.14. (2).

Karim, Maj. Gen. Afsir, "Editorial Perspective: Pakistan's Aggression in Kashmir: 1999 *Faultlines*, July 1999 Vol. 2. No. 4.

Karnad, Bharat, "A New Strategy for the LoC & Low-intensity Warfare in Kashmir", *Faultlines*, August 99, Vol. 2.

Karnad, Bharat, "Using LoC to India's Advantage", *Economic and Political Weekly*, Vol. KXXXIV, No.28, July 10,1999.

Katyal, K.K., "Stalemate in Indo-Pak. Talks," *The Hindu*, June 13, 1999.

Kaufmann, William W., "Limited Warfare," in *Military Policy and National Security*, eds. William W. Kaufmann et al. (Princeton, NJ: Princeton University Press, 1956)

Kaul, Air Chief Marshal S.K., "Talks, not adventurism will help Pak," *Hindustan Times*, 30 May 1999.

Khajuria, K.S., "The Line of Control in J & K as International Border?", *Aakrosh*, Vol.5, No.17, October 2002.

Khan, A.Q., "Pak Nuclear Scientist," Interview to 'Hurmat' *Strategic Digest*, Vol.25, No.6, June 1985, pp-679

Khan, Abdul Qadeer, "Indian Nuclear Policy and Pakistan Plan," *Strategic Digest*, Vol.25, No.12, December 1985, pp-1569

Khan, Tanvir Ahmad, "Managing the Kargil Crisis," *Dawn*, June 8, 1999.

Khanduri, Chandra B., "The Intrusion in Kargil," *Hindustan Times*, June 18, 1999

Kidwai, Saleem, "US Approach to Kargil: No Paradigm Shift in South Asia Policy", *Journal of Peace Studies*, Vol. 6, No.3, May-June, 1999.

Kissinger, Henry A., "Controls, Inspection and Limited War," *The Reporter* 16, no. 12 (June 13, 1957)

Kissinger, Henry, *Nuclear Weapons and Foreign Policy* (New York: Council on Foreign Relations, 1957), 139.

Kissinger, Henry, *The Necessity of Choice: Prospects of American Foreign Policy* (New York: Anchor Books, 1962)

Kolodziej, Edward A., "The Cold War as Cooperation," in *The Cold War as Cooperation: Superpower Cooperation in Regional Conflict Management*, eds. Roger E. Kanet and Edward A. Kolodziej (London: Macmillan, 1991)

Krishna, Maj. Gen. Ashok, "The Kargil War," in *Kargil: The Tables Turned*, eds.

Maj. Gen. Ashok Krishna and P.R. Chari, (New Delhi: Manohar Publishers, 2001): 88-95.

Kumar, Satish, "Making peace with India: Pakistan's Internal Imperatives", *USI Journal*, Vol XXXi, No.43, Jan-Mar 2001

Lancaster, John, "Kashmir Crisis Was Defused on the Brink of War," *Washington Post*, July 26, 1999.

Larson, Robert H., "B.H. Liddell Hart: Apostle of Limited War," *Military Affairs* 44, no. 2 (April 1980)

Malik, Gen. VP., "Indo-Pak Security Relations in the coming decade: Lessons from Kargil for the Future", *Indian Defence Review*, Vol.17 (1), January-March 2002.

Malik, Lt. Gen. N S., "Kargil-The End Game," *Agni*, February-May 1999, Vol.4, Number 2, PP-29-33

Manoj Joshi and Harinder Baweja, "Blasting Peace," *India Today* 24, no. 23 (June 7, 1999)

Manoj Joshi and Raj Chengappa, "The Marathon War," *India Today* 24, no. 25 (June 21, 1999)

Mateen, Amir, "Shahbaz Winds up US Visit," *The News*, May 17, 1999.

Mehmud, Khalid, "The Kargil Scenario," *The News*, June 3, 1999

Mehta, Maj. Gen. Ashok, "Let Army Decide on Safe Passage," *Hindustan Times*, June 4, 1999

Mian, Zia and Ramana, M V, "Beyond Lahore: From Transparency to Arms Control", *Economic and Political Weekly*, Vol. XXXIV, No.16-17, April17-24, 1999.

Mohan, Raja and Aneja, Atul, "Janus Faced Pakistan," *The Hindu*, June 13, 1999

Nair, Brigadier Vijai K "Indian Nuclear Doctrine: Domestic & External Challenges" *Agni*, February-May 1999, Vol. 4, no. 2.

Nambiar, Lt. Gen. Satish., "Command and Control Structure for Management of Nuclear Weapons" *Agni*, September 1998-January 1999, pp 1-13

Nasim Zehra, "Covert Contacts," *The News*, July 2, 1999.

Navlakha, Gautam, "Demilitarising Kargil: Urgent Tasks", *Economic and Political Weekly*, Vol. XXXIV, no.29, July 17,1999.

Navlakha, Gautam, "Kargil: Costs and consequences", *Economic and Political Weekly*, Vol. XXXIV, No.27, July 3, 1999.

Noorani, A.G., "An Aborted Deal," *Frontline* 16, no. 18 (September 10, 1999)

Noorani, A.G., "Kargil Diplomacy," *Frontline* 16, no. 16 (August 13, 1999).

Osgood, Robert E., *Limited War: The Challenge to American Strategy* (Chicago: The University of Chicago Press, 1957)

Patnaik, Elisa, "Tourism Slowly Picking up," *The Asian Age*, September 13, 1998

Perkovich, George, *India's Nuclear Bomb: The Impact on Global Proliferation* (Berkeley: University of California Press, 1999), 240-241.

Prakash, BG, "Operation Vijay Exposed Shortcomings: Indian Army Fought with A Broken Backbone", *Indian Defence Review*, Vol.16, No.4, October/December 2001.

Preston, Peter, "Musharraf: Our Short-term Friend and Long-term Enemy", *Peace Research*, Vol.34, No. 1, May 2002.

Punjabi, Riyaz, "Kargil Aggression: The Continuum of a Strategy", *Journal of Peace Studies*, Vol.6, No.3, May-June,1999.

Puri, Balraj, "A Post-Pokhran policy for Kashmir", *Economic and Political Weekly*, Vol. XXXIII, No.45, November 7, 1998.

Puri, Balraj, "India's Kargil Policy: Serious Flaws", *Economic and Political Weekly*, Vol. XXXIV, No.28, July 10, 1999.

Puri, Balraj, "India, Kashmir and War against Terrorism", *Economic and Political Weekly*, Vol. XXXVI, No.43, October 27, 2001.

Puri, Balraj, "Kashmir Problem Thrives on Denial of Human and Democratic Rights," *Economic and Political Weekly*, August 3, 1999, 795.

Puri, Balraj, "Peace in South Asia: Good Intentions and Ground Realities", *Economic and Political Weekly*, Vol.XXXVI, No.34, August 25,2001.

Qadir, Shaukat, "An Analysis of the Kargil Conflict 1999," *RUSI Journal* (April 2002).

Qazi, M.S., "High Tempers at High Mountains," *The Frontier Post*, June 7, 1999

Raghavan, V.R., "A Turning Point in Kashmir," *Frontline* 16, no. 12 (June 18, 1999).

Raghavan, V.R., "Military Persuasion or Provocation," *The Hindu*, February 12, 2003.

Raghavan, V.R., "More Than One Offensive Needed," *The Times of India*, June 8, 1999

Raghavan, V.R., "Strategic Pointers from Kargil," *The Hindu*, June 28, 1999.

Raghavan, V.R., "The Larger Purpose in Kargil," *The Hindu*, June 5, 1999

Raja, Maroof, "Pakistan-Sponsored Insurgency in Kasmir: A Case Study," *Faultlines*, July 1999, Vol. 2. No. 4.

Rajaraman, R, Ramana, M V and Mian, Zia, "Possession and Deployment of Nuclear weapons in South Asia: An Assessment of Some Risks", *Economic and Political Weekly*, Vol.37, No.25, June 22, 2002

Raman, B, "Covert Action and Counter Proxy War", *Indian Defence Review*, Vol.16, No.4, October/December 2001.

Raman, B, "The Kargil Operations," *Indian Defence Review*, April-June 99, Vol. 14 (2).

Raman, B., "Is Osama bin Laden in Kargil?" *The Indian Express*, May 26, 1999.

Rather, Ali Mohd. "Kargil: The Post-War Scenario," *Journal of Peace Studies* September-December 1999, Vol.6, nos.5&6.

Rehbein, Robert E., "Managing Proliferation in South Asia: A Case for Assistance to Unsafe Nuclear Arsenals", *The Nonproliferation Review*, Vol.9, No.1, Spring 2002

Rosen, Stephen Peter, "Vietnam and the American Theory of Limited War," *International Security* Vol.7, no. 2 (autumn 1982): 88.

Sachdev, A.K., "Media Related Lessons From Kargil," *Strategic Analysis*, January, 2000, Vol. XXIII, No. 10

Sagan, Scott D. and Kenneth N. Waltz, *The Spread of Nuclear Weapons: A Debate* (New York: W.W. Norton & Company, 1995)

Salik, Naeem Ahmad, "Missile Issues in South Asia", *The Nonproliferation Review*, Vol.9, No.2, Summer 2002.

Schelling, Thomas C., "Bargaining, Communication and Limited War," *Conflict Resolution* 1, no. 1 (March 1957)

Seshu, Geeta, "Media and Kargil: Information Blitz with Dummy Missiles",

Economic and Political Weekly, Vol. XXXIV, No.41, October 9, 1999.

Shaikh Shakil, "India Uses Weapons Akin to Nerve Gas Bombs," *The News*, May 27, 1999.

Shaikh, Shakil, "Pak Armed Forces Put on High Alert," *The News*, May 26, 1999.

Shaikh, Shakil, "PM, COAS Discuss Indian Build-up at LoC," *The News*, May 23, 1999.

Singh, Jasjit, "Dynamics of Limited War," *Strategic Analysis* (October 2000)

Singh, Jasjit, "Nuclear Command and Control", *Strategic Analysis*, Vol.XXV, No.2, May-2001.

Singh, Vikram Jit, "Kargil becoming another Siachen," *The Indian Express*, 31 May 1999

Subrahmanyam, K., "Advice for Mr. Aziz," *The Times of India*, June 7, 1999

Subrahmanyam, K., "Indo-Pak Nuclear Conflict Unlikely," *The Times of India*, January 2, 2002.

Swami, Praveen, "The Kargil War: Preliminary Explorations", *Faultlines*, August 99, Vol. 2

Swami, Praveen, "The Bungle in Kargil," *Frontline* 16, no. 13 (July 2, 1999).

Swami, Praveen, "War in Kargil," *Frontline* 16, no. 12 (June 18, 1999).

Syed Alamdar Raza, "Balance of Power in Kashmir," *The News*, June 3, 1999

Taubman, Philip, "Worsening India-Pakistan Ties Worry US," *The New York Times*, September 15, 1984.

Tellis, Ashley J., "The Strategic Implications of a Nuclear India", *Orbis*, Vol.46, no.1, Winter 2002.

Thomas, Lt Gen M, "Siachen After Kargil," *USI Journal*, Vol XXXi, No.43, Jan-Mar-2001.

Vanaik, Achin, "Nuclear Risk Reduction Measures Between India and Pakistan", *Economic and Political Weekly*, Vol.XXXVII, No.28, July 13, 2002.

Varadarajan, Siddharth, "Don't Escalate Kargil to All-out War," *The Times of India*, June 18, 1999

Vinayak, Ramesh, "Nasty Surprise," *India Today* (May 31, 1999): 21.

Waltz, Kenneth, *The Spread of Nuclear Weapons: More May Be Better*, Adelphi Paper 171 (London: IISS, 1981)

Wentz, Walter B., *Nuclear Proliferation* (Washington, DC: Public Affairs Press, 1968).

Winner, Andrew C. and Yoshihara, Toshi, "India and Pakistan at the Edge", *Survival*, Vol.44 no.3, Autumn 2002.

Wirsing, Robert G., *Kashmir in the Shadow of War: Regional Rivalries in a Nuclear Age* (Armonk, NY: M.E. Sharpe, 2003)

Index